VERSIONS of the SELF

Studies in English Autobiography

from John Bunyan

to John Stuart Mill

VERSIONS *of the* SELF

JOHN N. MORRIS

BASIC BOOKS, INC., PUBLISHERS
New York / London

Library of Congress Catalog Card Number: 66–13511
Manufactured in the United States of America
Designed by Florence D. Silverman

For nothing can be sole or whole
That has not been rent.

—W. B. Yeats

PREFACE

"Autobiography" is not an old word. If the O.E.D. is to be trusted, it first appeared in print in 1809, when Robert Southey used it in *The Quarterly Review*. The art itself was not new then, of course, even in England. Still, the invention of a new name for it and the immediate passage of that name into the standard vocabulary of English suggest that at that moment of invention the art was commanding a new sort of attention.

The grounds of that attention this study explores. The epigraph I have chosen from Yeats almost defines that modern conception of the self that assigns to pain a radical value. This notion has informed some remarkable lives. In the pages that follow I shall be chiefly concerned to examine the autobiographical accounts of a few of them, to the end of suggesting that these men were pioneers of the modern sensibility, unwitting agents of the new.

In writing this book I have been fortunate in enjoying the encouragement and guidance of Prof. James L. Clifford of Columbia University. I am indebted to Professors Quentin Anderson, Carl Woodring, Marshall Suther, and Herman Ausubel, also of Columbia, who read the manuscript and made many helpful suggestions. To the editors of *The American Scholar, Modern Age* and *The South Atlantic Quarterly* I am grateful for permission to reprint the chapters on Cowper, Gibbon and Bunyan.

PREFACE

I owe a prior debt to George Lyman Nesbitt and Thomas McNaughton Johnston, Professors of English, Hamilton College, and to them I offer this book.

JOHN N. MORRIS

New York City
March 1966

CONTENTS

VERSIONS of the SELF

I

INTRODUCTION

History is my subject here—personal history, the story of the self as certain autobiographers have told it. And history, of a very limited sort, is my object as well, for this study is intended to sketch the accession to intellectual respectability of a way of thinking—and therefore of writing—about oneself, a way now so nearly taken for granted that it is sometimes hard to remember that once people thought very differently about these matters. This way of thinking values the private and the inward in experience more highly than the public and the outward; it confers on events and feelings that are in no objective way verifiable a reality superior, at least in interest, to the reality of deeds and phenomena. In short, it is a way of thinking that helps to explain, because it helped to create, the difference between the eighteenth century on the one hand and the nineteenth and twentieth centuries on the other.

A statement of this sort is full of assumptions, and I had better be as open as possible about their nature. The chief among them has to do with the program of romanticism, the movement in literature and thought to the understanding of which this study aspires to contribute. This movement I take to have been in one of its aspects a response to the apparent meaninglessness of the world left to the first generation of romanticists by the men of the Enlightenment. The nature of this inherited wilderness is described by Robert Langbaum in the opening chapter of his admirable book, *The Poetry of Experience*.

> That wilderness is the legacy . . . of the scientific and critical effort of the Enlightenment which, in its desire to separate fact from the values of a crumbling tradition, separated fact from all values—bequeathing a world in which fact is measurable quantity while value is man-made and illusory. Such a world offers no objective verification for just the perceptions by which men live, perceptions of beauty, goodness and spirit. It was as literature began in the latter eighteenth century to realize the dangerous implications of the scientific world-view, that romanticism was born. It was born anew in at least three generations thereafter as men of genius arrived intellectually at the dead-end of the eighteenth century and then, often through a total crisis of personality, broke intellectually into the nineteenth. As literature's reaction to the eighteenth century's scientific world-view, romanticism connects the literary movements of the nineteenth and twentieth centuries.[1]

Thus, to separate fact from value is to be guilty of what Whitehead has called "the fallacy of misplaced concreteness"—the notion that mass, matter, figure, and extension are the only realities. Nature is, in this view, "a dull affair, soundless, scentless, colorless; merely the hurrying of material, endlessly, meaninglessly." [2] What it felt like to fall victim to such a view of the world the autobiographies of Wordsworth and John Stuart Mill describe. And their manner of passing out of this wilderness, the means of its redemption, Langbaum identifies in a phrase: "a total crisis of personality."

In this part, I shall examine Wordsworth's and Mill's autobiographies. There are several reasons for doing so. In the first place, these are works obviously worthy of attention in their own right. And, in the second place, the conception of how life feels as it is revealed in their pages still holds the stage. One purpose of my observations about these books is to suggest, sometimes by plain statement and sometimes by implication, that we still stand in something like their relationship to external reality and our own emotions. The similarities may be only the very general ones that, like them, we value highly and incline to live in our tutored feelings and that this high value and this inclination are conceived to be the signs of intelligence sensitized, deepened, and given access to wisdom by the experience of private neurotic suffering that approaches in intensity the "total crisis" of a Wordsworth or a Mill.

If I can convince the reader of this, I shall have gone far toward establishing the grounds of an interest in the books to which the later chapters of this study are devoted. For my principal assertion here is that the response of Wordsworth and Mill to the legacy of the Enlightenment, as they conceived or misconceived of it, had been anticipated in the eighteenth century and even earlier by a set of autobiographers outside the official literary culture. I mean John Bunyan and George Fox and a number of Quakers and Methodists and Evangelicals to whom the Enlightenment meant little or nothing, but who experienced in their own lives a spiritual dryness virtually indistinguishable as a felt thing from the deadness of the world and the affections so painfully familiar to Wordsworth and Mill. These men reconstituted and redeemed themselves (or suffered reconstitution and redemption) by undergoing their own total crises. For them it was a religious crisis, whereas for Wordsworth and Mill it was not, or not in a specifically Christian sense. But it felt the same. The experiences recorded in nineteenth-century autobiography are, I suggest, secular counterparts of the religious melancholy and conversions set down in the autobiographies of earlier heroes of religion.*

* Langbaum was painting with a broad brush in the passage quoted above, and so am I. No doubt it is possible to quarrel with his view and with my association of it with Whitehead's notions—notions that seem more clearly conformable to Wordsworth's misapprehension of reality at one point in his life than to Mill's. Mill was not depressed by the meaninglessness of nature and the world so much as by the apparent pointlessness of his own

Essentially, I am arguing that "self" is the modern word for "soul." The new way of thinking about oneself that I have said marks off the nineteenth from earlier centuries is new chiefly in being secular. One proposition this book seeks to affirm is that, if the modern sensibility is to be likened, however roughly, to the sensibility revealed in Wordsworth's and Mill's autobiographies, then that sensibility is at root religious. This proposition is convertible, of course. Perhaps I am saying no more than that the religious sensibility is a neurotic one—a notion boringly familiar in its ordinary acceptance. Still, it seems worth while to trace the continuity between the earlier and the later manifestations of this sensibility. That continuity is not a matter of influence or not influence first of all. There is no reason to believe that Mill or Wordsworth read Bunyan's autobiography or William Cowper's or, if they did, that their works were influenced by that reading.* I suggest only that the versions of the self—very different, no doubt, but more alike than different—recorded in Mill's *Autobiography* and *The Prelude* were anticipated by earlier men and that these versions were therefore somehow more easily available to Wordsworth and Mill.

"Somehow" is the operative word, of whose vagueness I am well aware. The manner in which the earlier styles of experience made themselves available to Wordsworth and Mill—and eventually and remotely to us—is a mystery I cannot penetrate. The self of any person must seem to him largely something given, not an object of choice. And, in any event, the experience of despair,

---

projects and ambitions. But, whatever Mill and Wordsworth were responding to, the responses themselves were much alike. Similarly, the occasions of the religious crises I shall be discussing may differ—from the occasions of Mill's crises and Wordsworth's and from one another—but subjectively the experiences of crisis are more alike than different.

* They *may* have read them or others that resembled them. Mill, as we shall see, explicitly likened his nervous collapse to the Methodist conviction of sin, and Wordsworth was much interested in Cowper. But it would be unwise to base an argument on these facts.

crisis, collapse, and rebirth is not something one would choose to imitate. But surely the chances that a consciousness will pursue a certain career are higher when that career is perceived, however dimly and by whatever means, to have served other men. I maintain that knowledge—intuited knowledge, perhaps—of the strategy of the religious for coping with the frightful realities of their own sinfulness and temptation to unbelief was available to Mill and Wordsworth, not only in books, but in the lives of their contemporaries. For the tone of the religious autobiographies and direct statements in some of them suggest that the experiences recorded there are conceived of as more nearly typical than extraordinary.

The writers describe what they suffered alone so that others might not be lonely in their suffering. The mode of feeling of these authors and of their mute audience a Wordsworth or a Mill imported into his own life, adapting it to his own circumstances and in turn helping to make it available to succeeding generations down to our own. It may be that this mode of feeling no longer serves. In us it may have reached the end of its usefulness. But what I am most concerned with is the nature of that mode of feeling as it is expressed in a number of autobiographies, some of them magnificent. The pretensions of this book to be a piece of history amount to this: I point to those autobiographers as the largely unacknowledged pioneers of the modern sensibility.*

* They are not, of course, *entirely* unacknowledged. For Hegel, "the modern time" began when men commenced "to force upon their souls the consciousness of their sinfulness and to know themselves as evil. The most simple souls, the most innocent natures were accustomed in painful introspection to observe the most secret workings of the heart, with a view to a rigid examination of them. With this duty was conjoined that of an entirely opposite description; it was required that a man should attain the consciousness that the good Spirit dwells in him—that Divine Grace has found an entrance into his soul. . . . Men became the victims of a tormenting uncertainty as to whether the good Spirit has an abode in them, and it was deemed indispensable that the entire process of spiritual transformation should become perceptible to the individual himself." The beginnings of this

My thesis, then, is that in the eighteenth century certain men were undergoing and valuing highly a kind of extreme and private experience that the representatives of the official culture could scarcely bring themselves to admit to consciousness, let alone find any virtue in. It was dangerous experience, and no doubt men like Dr. Johnson were right to shun it, for surely not everyone who underwent it survived. To a degree, the autobiographies of which I shall make so much give us a false picture, for they are the records of the undefeated. But the point is that, during the nineteenth century, consciousnesses capable of supporting such experience came more and more to predominate and to see in the suffering they had endured the source of that insight and wisdom that was their title to power. It seems to me that we still hold such notions, in however debased a form. It is true that we sometimes nowadays incline to value our acquaintance with the neurotic aspects of our constitution trivially, as a badge of a supposedly superior fineness of feeling. But we do value it. The knowledge to do so, I suggest, we owe partly to the men I shall be writing about in the chapters to follow. And from them we may yet learn—or learn again—something more. For what emerges from a study of these books is that what gives value to the experience of despair is the struggle to overcome it and that what makes direct knowledge of our irrational weaknesses morally interesting is that they may provoke in us the exercise of strength. These are didactic books; they teach us that it is our duty to be sane.

I have been speaking as though, aside from Mill's and Wordsworth's, the only autobiographies to be considered here are those

---

tendency Hegel associates with Luther and the early Reformation. But in England it found its voice in the religious autobiographies to be considered in these pages.—Georg Wilhelm Friedrich Hegel, *The Philosophy of History*, trans. J. Sibree (New York, 1956), pp. 424–425.

of Bunyan, Fox, Cowper, and the other chroniclers of religious experience; but that is not true. Part of my thesis is that autobiographies of this kind stand outside the main stream of eighteenth-century culture. To make that point clearly I must examine autobiographies that express the normal consciousness of the age. I do not mean the memoirs of travelers, criminals, actresses, and shopkeepers, which abounded in that century. They are interesting, no doubt, but I exclude them here, for they are beside my point. The autobiographies that express what I take to be the best standard consciousness of the age are two—Roger North's and Gibbon's. A man of family and affairs and a man of letters—together they stand for much of what is best in their times. The difference between these men and the religious writers, a difference I shall elaborate, is perhaps no more than this, that North and Gibbon exemplify the magnificent power of their culture to contain painful experience, whereas the religious autobiographers exemplify the more modern power to express it. Both kinds of power are admirable; but the second sort is the one that nowadays, for better or worse, seems the more necessary.

And finally I shall turn to Boswell. Strictly speaking, he is not an autobiographer. But in the many volumes of his journals we discover a consciousness that, though formed by the official culture, is in the grip of experience much like that undergone by the religious autobiographers whose pains he shared but without access to their comforts. The kinship we feel with Boswell—a kinship we cannot quite feel with Gibbon or North—establishes his modernity and should help to confirm my assertions about the sources of the modern sensibility.

Clearly, this study is a very partial, a very selective one. It does not pretend to be a historical survey of English autobiography, even in the century with which it is most concerned. Many names are omitted. Colley Cibber is not mentioned, nor is Laetitia Pilkington. I do not consider Benjamin Franklin, who, American though he was, might properly be judged an exemplar of the normal English consciousness of the age. I do not mention Rousseau's *Confessions*, a book whose example Gibbon acknowledged and which very likely influenced Wordsworth. And this study is partial in still another way. It does not attempt certain kinds of speculation; it does not adduce certain classes of fact. One might inquire what difference, if any, the age at which a man writes his autobiography makes. One might begin by examining closely the successive drafts of an autobiography—Wordsworth's, say, or Gibbon's—to see how increasing distance from an event modifies a man's account of it. These are interesting matters, but, since they lie outside the territory I have chosen to explore, I shall refer to them only in passing.

More questionably, perhaps, I have chosen to ignore the very real difficulty of ascertaining the truthfulness of these autobiographies. No doubt they are full of distortions. The final version of Mill's, for instance, as a recent edition of his first draft of it reveals, omits a great deal, partly for the reason that much of it passed under the relentless scrutiny of his wife.[3] And in neither version does he mention, except in the most guarded terms, his second nervous collapse, which afflicted him during the last year of his father's life. Conscious or unconscious, such suppressions must be highly significant. But significant of what? Did he "forget," or did he consciously suppress or transform an incident? Unless we can determine what part of the writer's mind accomplished the distortion, we cannot really understand its meaning. Hence I decline to draw many large conclusions from whatever inaccuracies I detect, and I adduce biographical information less often to correct an author's version of the facts than to amplify it. In short, I incline to accept his text—and not, I think, out of piety or laziness, but caution.

Autobiography is, as I have said, a species of history—a narrative of events occurring in time. At its simplest, it is a straightforward chronicle that begins at the beginning and proceeds, more or less mechanically, toward the present or whatever moment of termination the author has chosen. And yet the ordering of his experiences into a shape that answers better than mere continuous sequence to his notion of what his life really means is often one of the chief purposes of the autobiographer.

An example of a modern autobiography, *A Bundle of Sensations* (1961), by Goronwy Rees, should make my meaning clear. Here there is no attempt at continuity. The book consists of short narratives of events sometimes widely separated in time; these narratives present discrete and even contradictory versions of Rees's self. The lacunae and apparent inconsistencies are, however, not the results of the author's laziness or inattention; rather, they are the deliberate, formal expression of what Rees holds to be the truth about personality and in particular his own. It seems to him that, in a world where all is "chance, accident, absurdity," the notion of a "continuous personality which is identical with itself through all the changes it suffers in time" is an illusion and that hence conventional autobiography is a "trick." Experience offers, he says, only a "flux of impressions." [4]

Rees, it is clear, has moved away from the notion of how life feels that many of us, unreflectingly perhaps, still share with earlier autobiographers. My purpose at the moment, however, is not to dwell on that, but to suggest that *A Bundle of Sensations* is an obvious example of the fact that form in autobiography is as important a part of the meaning as it is in a poem or a novel and that, further, Rees's sense of the unconventionality of his work indicates something significant about the autobiographical tradition he distrusts. Form is also part of the meaning of the kind of autobiography against which he is protesting. Its narrative continuity asserts the unity of the self—that "continuous personality" that Rees denies.

It may be objected that every readable autobiography, like any other sensible account of events, displays some continuity or it is nothing; and that is true. But the interesting fact is that, in nineteenth-century autobiography, formal continuity is a principle of philosophic, not merely narrative, coherence. It is in some sense the emblem of the real subject of the work, the gradual evolution of an always-identifiable self. Psychological theory and philosophies of causation provided nineteenth-century writers with theoretical sanction for this view of themselves, a view that finds explicit verbal expression in the autobiographers' concern with the growth and development of the self.

Thus, John Stuart Mill proposes as one of the chief values of his *Autobiography* the fact that it notes "the successive phases" of a "mind which was always pressing forward," * and he tells us very little that does not bear on this subject. He habitually refers to his book as a "mental history," the record of his "mental progress," his "mental growth" and "development" (pp. 83, 93, 129, 132, 155, 161). The finest example of this kind of introspective autobiography is Wordsworth's long poem, *The Prelude*.

The Prelude is the magnificent exception to the rule that English poets of the first rank do not write good autobiographies or any autobiographies at all. Oddly enough, this poem—perhaps because it *is* a poem—is often slighted in studies of autobiography. And yet *The Prelude* is a most successful attempt to reduce the chaos of experience to intelligible order and to find in that order transcendent significance.

Wordsworth composed *The Prelude*, he tells us, as part of the "review of his own mind" that he undertook in order to determine whether he was capable of conceiving "a literary work that might live." † The striking fact is that the form this "review"

* John Stuart Mill, *Autobiography*, ed. John Jacob Coss (New York, 1924), p. 1. Subsequent citations of this work will mention only the page number and will appear in the text, in parentheses.

† William Wordsworth, *The Prelude*, ed. Ernest de Selincourt; 2d ed., rev. Helen Darbishire (Oxford, 1959), p. 509. Unless otherwise noted, citations of the poem will be to the 1850 version and will appear in the text, in parentheses.

assumes is not an inventory of his present stock of ideas but an inquiry into their origins. This placid assumption that a mind and its contents are best understood in terms of their genesis and growth is, of course, what turns the "review" into an autobiography. And Wordsworth's concern with the continuous development of a self commits him to a philosophy of becoming.

Thus, in *The Prelude*, Wordsworth treasures a sense of personal incompleteness, for it holds promise for the future. The soul, he says, aspires toward "possible sublimity"

> With faculties still growing, feeling still
> That whatsoever point they gain, they yet
> Have something to pursue.
> (II, 320–322)

The greatest disaster is fulfillment, which constitutes a kind of death. He grieves to see Mont Blanc, though he had been traveling toward it, presumably on purpose. Its "soulless image" had

> usurped upon a living thought
> That never more could be.
> (VI, 527–528)

When at last he crosses the Alps, he is depressed to discover that, though he still "had hopes that pointed to the clouds" (VI, 587), his "future course . . . was downward" (VI, 584–585). The meaning of this experience is at the moment obscure to him. As he writes *The Prelude*, however, its significance becomes clear.

> Our destiny, our being's heart and home,
> Is with infinitude, and only there;
> With hope it is, hope that can never die,
> Effort, and expectation, and desire,
> And something evermore about to be.
> (VI, 604–608)

Effort, expectation, desire, but not the "spoils" and "trophies" (VI, 610); struggle and aspiration, but not achievement—these are the proper business of the soul. The "woods decaying, never to be decayed, / The stationary blasts of waterfalls" (VI, 625–626) are outward and visible signs that life is process without end, an eternity of change.

These ideas are expressed, not in isolated passages only, but in Wordsworth's very conception of the whole poem as an emblem of his life. That is to say, an image he uses to convey his sense of the poem as a work coincides with one of the several images he uses for the life the poem recapitulates. Expressing continuity, vigor, and growth, it is, as we might expect, an image drawn from nature, a river. Sometimes it represents the poem only, as when Wordsworth says that the very earliest lines—the "glad preamble"—came from him "like a torrent bursting" and were followed by "a less impetuous stream" that, after flowing a while, "stopped for years" (VII, 6–11). Sometimes the river stands only for his life; it proceeded, he tells us from its source in a "blind cavern," was "engulphed" for a time, and has at last reappeared to flow on strongly and steadily (XIV, 195–202). On occasion, however, the river represents both his life and the poem at once. Thus, at the beginning of Book IX, when he is about to speak of his residence in France and the emotional distress that followed, Wordsworth writes that, in composing *The Prelude,* he has "Turned and returned with intricate delay" (IX, 8)

> Even as a river,—partly (it might seem)
> Yielding to old remembrances, and swayed
> In part by fear to shape a way direct,
> That would engulph him soon in the ravenous sea—
> Turns and will measure back his course, far back,
> Seeking the very regions which he crossed
> In his first outset. . . .
>
> (IX, 1–7)

As an autobiographer, Wordsworth is not, as it were, separate from himself and his past. One does not retrace the river of one's life; really, it retraces itself. The process of life is dynamic; it will not pause to be examined. Moments of retrospection themselves become immediately part of that past of which one is attempting to make sense.*

Here, then, is something new—the notion that the very composition of the autobiography of a life conceived of as process and flow is in itself an act that may be as privately and vividly important as any of the experiences set down. For Wordsworth, indeed, composing *The Prelude* had consequences more important than those of any single event recalled. Speaking again of his life as a river, he asserts that

> from its progress have we drawn
> The feeling of life endless, the great thought
> By which we live, Infinity and God.†

From its progress, that is, from discovering through recollection life's unity and flow, Wordsworth has penetrated to the "great thought" that gives meaning to human existence: the notion that our life considered as a progress is the emblem of a metaphysical fact—the continuity of this world and the next in terms of movement forever onward. This conception allows Wordsworth

* This is at last a kind of trap for the autobiographer, if he goes too far with it. Like the narrator of *Tristram Shandy*, he will never catch up with the present, no matter how many volumes he issues.

† These lines from the 1805 version (XIII, 203–205) Wordsworth revised to read

> from its progress have we drawn
> Faith in life endless, the sustaining thought
> Of human Being, Eternity, and God.

Essentially the point is the same, though "sustaining thought" is a weaker expression than "the great thought / By which we live." The effect is to make the utterance more acceptably orthodox, as in the substitution of "Eternity" for the theologically neutral "Infinity."

to explain to himself the experience he had had crossing the Alps. Our destiny is indeed "with infinitude"; our "future course" is not, as he had been tempted to conclude, "forever downward." This confidence Wordsworth owes to writing *The Prelude*. The very high claim that the act of retrospection and composition is in itself the source of a knowledge higher than the particular truths of the experiences recorded marks Wordsworth's autobiography off from all previous English examples of the form.

It is not to that "great thought"—or not *directly* to it—that we must look to find a connection between *The Prelude* and other autobiographies. The point of contact is rather the despondency that overcame him after his stay in France during the Revolution—a despondency that in its felt quality closely resembles the intense depression known at some time in their lives by such diverse intellectual figures as Mill, Carlyle, and Newman in England, Tolstoy in Russia, and William James in America. Wordsworth's account of his "mental crisis"—Mill's phrase for it—is a paradigm of the experience. Further, as we shall see, he prescribed and could himself provide a cure.

That Wordsworth's mental depression was very painful *The Prelude* leaves no doubt. It was most intense during 1795, but it may have had its beginnings earlier, perhaps during Wordsworth's visit to Paris in October 1792. Then and for some time to come, Wordsworth's enthusiasm for the French Revolution was high; yet, he tells us, he could not help thinking of "those September massacres, / Divided from me by one little month" X, 73–74). A few weeks earlier, the citizens of Paris, having been called out to relieve besieged Verdun, had under pressure of military necessity in four days executed, with or without trial, some eleven hundred prisoners whom they had feared to leave behind in the city. To Wordsworth these executions seemed murders. In the light of day, Wordsworth was able to think of them as "Ephemeral monsters, to be seen but once"; as he lay reading in his room at night, however, "the fear gone by / Pressed on me almost like a fear to come."

> For the spent hurricane the air provides
> As fierce a successor; the tide retreats
> But to return out of its hiding place
> In the great deep; all things have second birth;
> The earthquake is not satisfied at once;
> And in this way I wrought upon myself
> Until I seemed to hear a voice that cried,
> To the whole city, "Sleep no more." . . .
> The place, all hushed and silent as it was,
> Appeared unfit for the repose of night,
> Defenceless as a wood where tigers roam.
>
> (X, 46, 71–93)

The Terror, beginning just one year after the September massacres, constituted that fierce successor Wordsworth had feared. For years afterward, his sleep was troubled by dreams in which he vainly pled before "unjust tribunals" and felt a sense of "treacherous desertion . . . / In the last place of refuge—my own soul" (X, 411–415). Already divided against himself by England's declaration of war against France (XI, 173–185), he now felt himself betrayed by the cause with which he had been in sympathy. Although he was able to persuade himself that the Terror was no more than a purging of the Old Regime's "terrific reservoir of guilt" (X, 477), his faith in the Revolution was weakened.

Now, vainly, he summoned his "best skill" and "toiled, intent / To anatomise the frame of social life" and search "the whole body of society" to its heart (XI, 279–282). At last, in 1795, having dragged "all precepts, judgments, maxims, creeds, / Like culprits to the bar" (XI, 294–295), Wordsworth lost

> All feeling of conviction, and, in fine,
> Sick, wearied out with contrarieties,
> Yielded up moral questions in despair.

This was the crisis of that strong disease,
This the soul's last and lowest ebb.
(XI, 303–307)

An intimation of how far he felt himself to have strayed from his true course is implicit in the images he uses for himself in those lines: he has been more surgeon and lawyer than poet.

He had been turned aside, he tells us, "From Nature's way by outward accidents" (XI, 291). As he understood by the time he came to write *The Prelude,* the next step was not surprising.

What wonder, then, if to a mind so far
Perverted, even the visible Universe
Fell under the dominion of a taste
Less spiritual, with microscopic view
Was scanned, as I had scanned the moral world?
(XII, 88–92)

The adjective "microscopic" is revealing. Here is "the fallacy of misplaced concreteness." The world is dead, it now seems to Wordsworth, and his early experiences of it have told him only lies; what the mind "half creates" is nonsense. Since the seventeenth century, one of the great tasks of the imagination has been to combat this misconception. Wordsworth would do so—when he had recovered.

His recovery was gradual, and I do not mean to detail it here. In brief, he rediscovered the significance of the fact that

The morning shines,
Nor heedeth Man's perverseness; Spring returns,—
I saw the Spring return, and could rejoice. . . .
(XII, 31–33)

"All things have second birth," he had said, brooding on the September Massacres; the lesson that he now drew from that fact was no longer a melancholy one.

The political events of which Wordsworth speaks in the passages just considered may have been the occasion of his depression; but surely they were not, by themselves, the cause. We nowadays believe that, to find the cause of such a psychic episode, we must look to moments more remote. What they were, Wordsworth (whether out of reticence or ignorance) does not say. But he does specify moments whose recollection helped to work his recovery. As is well known, his sense of a "renovating virtue" in the memory of certain "spots of time" (XII, 208–210) contributed greatly to this reconversion. Those moments in his past seem to him full of meaning, though precisely *what* meaning is incommunicable and, except in a very general sense, unclear even to Wordsworth.

What *is* certain, however, is that "science" can find no meaning in them at all. The noumenality of these experiences and their very vagueness of import convince, or reconvince, Wordsworth of the reality of things invisible to the "microscopic view." It seems to him once again that "The mind is lord and master—outward sense / The obedient servant of her will" (XII, 222–223). The stream of his experience of nature had for a time been "engulphed," but now it rose again "In strength, reflecting from its placid breast / The works of man and face of social life" (XIV, 199–202). A view of nature as the "image of right reason" (XIII, 22) and the source of moral ideas succeeded, but did not displace, the earlier view of nature as a source of joy. Memory, called forth by the enervating influence of mental crisis, united in the experience of the present moment all stages of his mental progress and confirmed him in that sense of the unity and integrity of his experience that would suggest to him the "great thought by which we live."

The effect of his despondency was, at last, to deepen his trust in his feelings. They had "stood the test" of a severe trial (XIII, 56–57), and their strength and rightness were thus established more firmly than ever. This is most important, for what is new and interesting in the experience of Wordsworth and the others who, as I have said, suffered similar periods of gloom and despondency is not the ordeal itself, but the value they put on it. A comment of Mill's on this matter is typical in its mixture of gratitude and anguish. "At all events," he wrote to Carlyle in 1833, "I will not, if I can help it, give way to gloom and morbid despondency, of which I have had a large share in my short life, and to which I have been indebted for all the most valuable of such insight as I have into the most important matters; neither will this return of it be without similar fruits, as I hope and almost believe." [5]

So valuable, indeed, did such experience eventually seem that, by the twentieth century, William James was asserting in *The Varieties of Religious Experience* that *only* the "sick soul," the "divided self" who has "in his own person become the prey of a pathological melancholy," can know the world for what it is.[6] "Crocodiles and rattlesnakes and pythons are at this moment vessels of life as real as we are," James insists; ". . . and whenever they or other wild beasts clutch their living prey, the deadly horror which an agitated melancholic feels is the literally right reaction on the situation." [7] To see how far the nineteenth century has taken us, we may oppose to James's notions the fairly clear idea of the best orthodox eighteenth-century view of the value of private experience that may be gleaned from Boswell's *Life*. Johnson was no more a stranger to what in *Rasselas* he calls "the tyranny of reflection" than any of the sufferers whose experiences James describes. In 1729 (at almost the same time as his conversion to an active Christian faith) and intermittently thereafter, Johnson was "overwhelmed with an horrible hypochondria, with perpetual irritation, fretfulness, and impatience; and with a dejection, gloom, and despair, which made existence misery." *

* Boswell's *Life of Johnson*, ed. George Birkbeck Hill and revised and enlarged by L. F. Powell (Oxford, 1934), I, 63–64. Johnson, to be sure, re-

Nowhere, however, does Johnson advance the view that a merely private experience is a trustworthy source of knowledge for anyone, or about anything, but the man who has undergone the experience. Of the Methodists' "inward light," for instance, he remarks: "If a man pretends to a principle of action of which I can know nothing, nay, not so much as that he has it; how can I tell what that person may be prompted to do?" [8] Private experience is here seen as a likely source of error and an easy refuge for the intellectual scoundrel. Johnson's view of the world is fully as somber as James's, but the notion that a crisis of despondency is a prerequisite to moral insight would have been abhorrent to him.

The title of James's book and the appositeness of Johnson's views on Methodism suggest one link I spoke of earlier in this chapter between these nineteenth-century intellectuals and the Dissenters of earlier times. What occurs in even so secular a mind as Mill's during his mental crisis is something remarkably like religious conversion. In the accounts of such experiences, there are often three stages (which Carlyle calls "The Everlasting No," "The Center of Indifference," and "The Everlasting Yea") [9] through which the "divided self" of the "sick soul" (to use James's terms again) must pass. Thus, Wordsworth, repelled by the course of contemporary history, "Yielded up moral questions in despair", sank into an apathy in which the very world seemed lifeless and blank; and at last, under the influence of nature and memory, emerged, strengthened and renewed, as one of the

---

mained always a "divided self." He "never [after 1729] was perfectly relieved" of his mental depression, and "all his labours, and all his enjoyments, were but temporary interruptions of its baleful influence." His conversion, a fully religious one that followed his reading of Law's *Serious Call*, was more an act of faith and will than it was that radical reordering of the mind and emotions, that unification of the self, of which others speak; indeed, it preceded, rather than followed, the onset of his melancholia. (See Boswell's *Life*, I, 68). Johnson, nevertheless, is the best eighteenth-century example we have of a man who, having endured at least a part of this experience, denied it any value.

"twice-born." Such an experience comes, as James makes clear in the passages I have quoted, to distinguish the intellectually elect from the "once-born and their sky-blue optimistic gospel" as clearly as religious conversion is supposed to distinguish the saved from the damned.[10]

An examination of Mill's account of this experience should make the matter clear. It parallels Wordsworth's; indeed, Mill himself asserts the similarity.

Mill writes in his *Autobiography* of the moment when, in his twenty-first year, his mental crisis began:

> It was in the autumn of 1826. I was in a dull state of nerves, such as anybody is occasionally liable to; unsusceptible to enjoyment or pleasurable excitement; one of those moods when what is pleasure at other times, becomes insipid or indifferent; the state, I should think, in which converts to Methodism are, when smitten by their first "conviction of sin" (p. 94).

The comparison stated in the last part of this sentence, the climax toward which the particulars of the preceding phrases tend, is a suggestive piece of self-analysis. Its weight is the more impressive for its coming from a man who never had and never wished to have any religious belief. Subsequent chapters of this study will pursue the hint that it offers us.

For Mill (as, indeed, for Methodists) this was only the beginning. "In this frame of mind," he goes on to say,

> it occurred to me to put the question directly to myself: "Suppose that all your objects in life were realized; that all the changes in institutions and opinions which you are looking forward to, could be completely effected at this very moment: would this be a great joy and happiness to you?" And an irrepressible self-consciousness distinctly answered, "No!" At this my heart sank within me: the whole foundation on which my life was constructed fell down. All my happiness was to have been found in the continual pur-

> suit of this end. The end had ceased to charm, and how could there ever again be any interest in the means? I seemed to have nothing left to live for (p. 94).

Why had that "irrepressible self-consciousness" answered as it had? Mill's explanation is that he had become the victim of his own analytic powers. He had been taught by his father to believe that "all mental and moral feelings and qualities . . . were the results of association and that the formation of salutary associations was therefore the object of education" (pp. 95–96). Now he discerned that there was something "artificial and casual" in the associations that his father, by "the old, familiar instruments, praise and blame," had formed in him (p. 96). To Mill, such associations seemed now to lack the strength "to resist the dissolving influence of analysis, while the whole course of my intellectual cultivation had made precocious and premature analysis the inveterate habit of my mind" (p. 97). This habit of analysis, he now saw, "has a tendency to wear away the feelings . . . when no other mental habit is cultivated, and the analysing spirit remains without its natural complements and correctives" (p. 96).

The qualifying force of those last two clauses must not be missed. Mill is far from denying the value of the kind of education he received. If, in an excess of sympathy for the boy who could not remember the time when he knew no Greek, we suppose that the sole cause of his despondency was the dry rigor of his studies, we should remember that those studies had provided him the only moments of intense happiness he had so far enjoyed. The reading of "Bentham's principal speculations," for instance, had opened up for the fifteen-year-old Mill a "vista of improvement . . . sufficiently large and brilliant to light up my life" (pp. 46–48). The failure of his education lay in sacrificing to the "training of the human being for speculation and action" the cultivation of the "passive susceptibilities" (pp. 100–101). What had brought on the crisis was not too much of one kind of education, but too little of another.*

Whatever the reason, Mill had now reached that depth of depression that Carlyle had named "The Everlasting No." The world seemed dead, as it had to Wordsworth at the corresponding moment in his history. Carlyle's description of this period of his own distress sums it up.

> Now when I look back, it was a strange isolation I then lived in. The men and women around me, even speaking with me, were but Figures. . . . To me the Universe was all void of Life, of Purpose, of Volition, even of Hostility; it was one huge, dead, immeasurable Steam-engine, rolling on, in its dead indifference, to grind me limb from limb.[11]

This deadness of the world was a corollary of the barrenness of Mill's self. Every morning he

> awoke to a renewed consciousness of the woeful fact. I carried it with me into all companies, into all occupations. . . . I was . . .

* Moreover, Mill's education was not quite so mercilessly devoted to useful knowledge as the casual reader of his *Autobiography* sometimes supposes. James Mill was no Thomas Gradgrind. The Mills enjoyed long family vacations at Bentham's house in Devonshire, a building whose architecture gave young John "the sentiment of a larger and freer existence and [was] to me a sort of poetic cultivation" (p. 39). He acquired a taste for natural scenery, which, strengthened by a visit to the Pyrenees during his year in France, "gave a colour to my tastes through life" (p. 40). The books he read were not all deadly serious. He enjoyed *Robinson Crusoe*, *The Arabian Nights,* and various accounts of famous voyages, and he claimed Fielding and Goldsmith as influences on his prose style (pp. 6, 82). Though he did not care for much poetry, he used to "sing internally, to a music of my own," Dryden's "Alexander's Feast" and some of Scott's songs (p. 12); he liked Pope's translation of the *Iliad* and even composed one book of a continuation of it (p. 10). And he obtained, he says, "poetic culture of the most valuable kind, by means of reverential admiration for the lives and characters of heroic persons: especially the heroes of philosophy." But all this was not enough. As far as his father, James Mill, was concerned, such poetic culture "could take care of itself"; although the ground was prepared, it was not (in Mill's word) "cultivated" (pp. 77, 79).

> left stranded at the commencement of my voyage, with a well-equipped ship and a rudder, but no sail; without any real desire for the ends I had been so carefully fitted out to work for: no delight in virtue, or the general good, but also just as little in anything else. The fountains of vanity and ambition seemed to have dried up within me, as completely as those of benevolence (pp. 94, 97–98).

Mill felt, as Wordsworth said of himself, "inwardly oppressed" with

> vexing thoughts
> Confusion of the judgment, zeal decayed
> And, lastly, utter loss of hope itself
> And things to hope for.
> (XII, 3–7)

He had been cut off from that direct experience of ideas that had once been the sure source of the kind of happiness he had known on first reading Bentham. He knew, he says, that, if he could once again feel the force of those ideas, of whose truth he was still intellectually convinced, all would be well; "but to know that a feeling would make me happy if I had it, did not give me the feeling" (p. 98). "What availed," asked Wordsworth, speaking to the same point,

> When spells forbade the voyager to land,
> The fragrant notice of a pleasant shore . . . ?
> (XII, 52–54)

For months to come, Mill's energies were to be directed toward the apparently hopeless task of creating "in a mind now irretrievably analytic, fresh associations with any of the objects of human desire" (p. 98). Those fresh associations were, as we shall see, to be natural ones, not the "artificial and casual" ones imposed on him during his education.

Not until the following spring did Mill begin to recover. Like Carlyle, who said of the moments on Leith Walk in Edinburgh when he defied "The Everlasting No," "Perhaps I directly thereupon began to be a man." [12] Mill, after being moved to tears by the account in Marmontel's *Mémoires* of how the author had as a boy made his family feel that he would "supply the place" of his dead father, could believe that he was "not a stock or stone. . . . I gradually found," he says, "that the ordinary incidents of life could again give me some pleasure" (p. 99). Mill passed now into a period of moderate happiness darkened by "several relapses, some of which lasted many months" (p. 99).* Again Carlyle's words for his own plight describe Mill's:

> Wretchedness was still wretched; but I could now partly see through it, and despise it. . . . This . . . was the CENTER OF INDIFFERENCE I had now reached; through which whoso travels from the Negative Pole to the Positive must necessarily pass.[13]

"I had now learnt by experience," Mill writes, "that the passive susceptibilities needed to be cultivated as well as the active capacities" (p. 101). Mill could still feel; in some sense, as Michael St. John Packe suggests,[14] he was now feeling more acutely than ever. The trouble was that what he was feeling was the barrenness of the self. The experience of ideas was inaccessible, and he was only mildly sensitive to those other influences

* A. S. Levi, in "The 'Mental Crisis' of John Stuart Mill," *The Psychoanalytic Review*, XXXII (January 1945), 86–101, attributes Mill's crisis to the almost total moral domination his father had exercised over him. Quoting an early draft of the *Autobiography* in which Mill wrote, "I acquired a habit of leaving my responsibility as a moral agent to rest on my father and my conscience never speaking to me except by his voice," Levi concludes that, resenting this domination, Mill felt, but repressed, a wish for his father's death. The "psychic energy" this repressed, says Levi, "found its substitute expression—and this substitute expression was just the sum of his neurotic symptoms!" The passage from Marmontel began his cure by bringing his repressed feelings to "full consciousness through speech, action, or imagination," thus discharging them.

that give pleasure. He had now to stimulate that faint sensitivity. All his thoughts and inclinations, he says, "turned in an increasing degree toward whatever seemed capable of being instrumental toward that object" (p. 101). It was to Wordsworth that, at last, he turned.

Mill did not come on Wordsworth's poems until the autumn of 1828, a year and a half after the first slight easing of his depression that his reading of Marmontel had provided. If we are to understand the relief those poems supplied him, we must be aware of the desperate loneliness that had attended his despondency from its onset. He had felt from the first, he writes, "that mine was not an interesting, or in any way respectable distress. Advice, if I had known where to seek it, would have been most precious." Recourse to his father was impossible:

> I saw no use in giving him the pain of thinking that his plans had failed, when the failure was probably irremediable, and, at all events, beyond the power of *his* remedies. Of other friends I had at that time none to whom I had any hope of making my condition intelligible (p. 95).

It was in something like this state of mind that Mill, out of curiosity rather than hope, dipped into the 1815 collection of Wordsworth's poems and found, in the "Ode: Intimations of Immortality from Recollections of Early Childhood," proof or what he held to be proof that the poet "had had similar experience to mine; that he also had felt that the first freshness of youthful enjoyment of life was not lasting; but that he had sought for compensation, and found it," in the way in which the other poems in the volume could teach Mill to find it (pp. 104–105). Here was the precious advice he had needed.

During the two years between the onset of his depression and his reading of Wordsworth, Mill had come to suspect that the flaw in his happiness was "a flaw in life itself," and that, if the aims of the reformers were accomplished, mankind, no longer under the necessity of struggle, would find that the pleasures of life had ceased to be pleasures (p. 102). For this final difficulty, which Mill had to overcome if he was to emerge from his despondency, Wordsworth had the answer. His poems, Mill says, were for him "the very culture of the feelings, which I was in quest of"; but, even more important, they seemed

> a source of inward joy, of sympathetic and imaginative pleasure, which could be shared in by all human beings; which had no connexion with struggle or imperfection, but would be made richer by every improvement in the physical or social condition of mankind. From them I seemed to learn what would be the perennial sources of happiness, when all the greater evils of life shall have been removed.

For public as well as private reasons, therefore, he felt "at once better and happier as I came under their influence" (p. 104).

Mill's depression now gradually passed away. Under Wordsworth's influence, his mind formed those "'fresh associations" with "the objects of human desire" that he had once almost despaired of establishing. The ends to which he had devoted his mind before the crisis became again attractive. Mill's reading of Wordsworth now convinced him that what his father's training had once rendered artificially and temporarily desirable had a real and permanent connection with the private happiness of the individual. For a time at least, Mill's spirits were restored.*

* William James, too, suffered a severe depression which seemed to him to have its source in what he took to be the excessive abstractness of his intellectual preoccupations. "To make the *form* of all possible thought the prevailing *matter* of one's thought breeds hypochondria," he wrote in his diary. When he recovered ("It's the difference between death and life," he told his father), the elder Henry James asked what had brought about the change; William replied that his cure had been worked partly by reading Wordsworth, "whom he [had] been feeding on now for a good while." *The Letters of William James*, ed. Henry James [III] (Boston, 1920), I, 168–170.

Mill hoped, he said in that letter to Carlyle quoted earlier, that his despondency would not return; but, if it did, he could "almost believe" that it would provide more of that "most valuable of such insight as I have into the most important matters." The fact is that, for Wordsworth, Mill, and others, a crisis of the sort described here and the insight it brought seem to have been a necessary prelude to their achievements. They learned that the power of an experience resides less in the event than in the response to it. The world and life had meaning only in their experience of it, and that depended on the vigor of the self. The self could die, they discovered, and, when it did, the world died with it. Recovery was not a mere reversion to natural health but, like Christian conversion, a rebirth to a new world. Self-consciousness they knew to be, in Mill's phrase, "the daemon of the men of genius of our time," and to that self-consciousness the age owed "much both of its cheerful and its mournful wisdom." [15]

Thus, Mill's despondency and his recovery from it were the occasion of his grounding firmly in the self his projects for the improvement of society—projects that became, in time, quite different from those for which his father and Bentham had worked. And *On Liberty*, the book on which (as he foresaw) his modern reputation largely rests, would perhaps never have been written if he had not suffered as he did; for the power, he says, "by which one human being enters into the mind and circumstances of another" [16]—the imagination that, finding room for human diversity, is present everywhere in *On Liberty*—is impossible for the healthy-minded to attain. For Wordsworth, too, the reordering of conceptions that mental crisis entailed had important consequences. It forced him to perceive that the sources of his moral ideas were not the abstract speculations of other men, but nature and his recollections of his early, intuitive responses to it. That perception is at the heart of most of his poems that we remember, few of which had been written before his despondency.

That perception, rising out of his "heart-experience," is a source of his poetic power, and that power, as Mill testifies, was sanative. Mill was wrong about precisely how his experience resembled Wordsworth's, but it made no difference.* For Mill did not learn to feel from reading *The Prelude*, where the poet deals directly with his own distress. The poems that taught Mill were not written *about* Wordsworth's sufferings, but as a *result* of them—according, that is, to a theory of poetry as a therapeutic agent at which Wordsworth's crisis had helped him to arrive.

Matthew Arnold was right. The supreme virtue of Wordsworth's poetry is its "healing power." [17] What Arnold finds in the poems is precisely what Mill found: their capacity to "make us feel," freeing souls from "the prison-cell / Of festering thoughts" and the "benumbing round" of modern life.[18] Something like this is the meaning of Arnold's widely misunderstood dictum in his essay on Wordsworth (and elsewhere) that poetry is "a criticism of life." The "lesson," so to speak, of "The Solitary Reaper" has nothing directly to do with the explicit content of the poem; the Highland lass is not being criticized, the *reader* is, on the ground that, caught in the "benumbing round," he is, in his incapacity or unwillingness to feel, leading a less than human life.† Poetry is to be understood first in terms of its effects, not its statements.

* Mill was slightly off the mark in believing that the similarity between his case and Wordsworth's lay in the fact that the poet, like himself, had "felt that the first freshness of youthful enjoyment of life was not lasting" (p. 105). It was not so simple as that, for either of them.

† See Lionel Trilling's essay "Wordsworth and the Rabbis" in his *The Opposing Self*, New York, 1959, p. 136. "Matthew Arnold said that in a wintry clime, in an iron time, Wordsworth taught us to *feel*. This statement, extreme as it is, will be seen to be not inaccurate if we bring to mind the many instances of spiritual and psychological crisis in the nineteenth century in which affectlessness, the loss of the power to feel, played an important part. *Ennui*, *noia*—how often we meet with them in nineteenth-century biography; and the *acedia* which was once a disorder of the specifically religious life becomes now a commonplace of secular spirituality."

There can be no doubt that Wordsworth intended his poems to be *used*. In the "Preface" to the 1800 edition of *Lyrical Ballads*, he proposes his poems as an antidote for the "savage torpor" contemporary life produced in many.[19] Wordsworth believed that he had himself escaped from that torpor and from the "prison-cell" by returning, in act and recollection, to a trustful intercourse with the natural world. Writing *The Prelude* was the last step in his recovery. As he composed, he found that

> The days gone by
> Return upon me almost from the dawn
> Of life: the hiding-places of man's power
> Open; I would approach them, but they close.
> I see by glimpses now; when age comes on,
> May scarcely see at all. . . .
>
> (XII, 277–282)

Before those "hiding-places" closed forever, Wordsworth wished to give

> Substance and life to what I feel, enshrining,
> Such is my hope, the *Spirit of the Past*
> *For future restoration.*
>
> (XII, 284–286)

My emphasis serves only to draw attention to the words in which his meaning most explicitly resides. He here intends the poetic record of his early life to have a therapeutic effect, a "renovating virtue" (XII, 210) as pure and almost as powerful as nature itself. Wordsworth hopes to find in *The Prelude* the same thing that Mill found in the 1815 edition of his poems.

Rightly considered, Wordsworth tells us, poetry is a natural force. He had learned of

> the great Nature that exists in works
> Of mighty poets. Visionary power

Attends the motions of the viewless winds,
Embodied in the mystery of words. . . .
(V, 594–597)

His highest hope is that

a work of his
Proceeding from a source of untaught things
Creative and enduring, may become
A power like one of Nature's.
(XIII, 309–312)

He does not wish to be a "Poet only to myself, to men / Useless" (X, 233–234). Nature has shaped, cherished, and restored him, and he, in his verse, will do the same for other men. Now his natural metaphors for himself take on a new and larger meaning. In writing *The Prelude,* he tells us at the poem's close,

I rose
As if on wings, and saw beneath me stretched
Vast prospect of the world which I had been
And was.
(XIV, 379–382)

Out of this world came the poems that served Mill as the real world had served Wordsworth.

Surely Roy Pascal is speaking for the modern reader when, in *Design and Truth in Autobiography,* he writes:

> The life is represented in autobiography not as something established but as a process; it is not simply the narrative of the voyage, but also the voyage itself. There must be in it a sense of discovery, and where this is wanting, and the autobiography appears as an exposition of something understood from the outset, we feel it a failure, a partial failure at any rate.[20]

Judged by this standard, *The Prelude* is a tremendous success. In composing it, as we have seen, Wordsworth discovered the very process of recurring to his past and setting it down to be a source of strength and an instrument of knowledge about what he held to be a transcendent truth—that "great thought" on which we dwelt earlier. The latter aspect of his researches into himself—their metaphysical import—many today would not value. But the wish to discover in one's past a personal, subjective meaning is still with us.

Indeed, Pascal's description of the interest in himself which preceded his writing a scholarly work on autobiography summarizes part of Wordsworth's motive. He felt that "one could be content," he writes, "if one could feel one's self to be consistent, to have developed naturally and organically, to have remained 'true to itself,' and if within this framework one could order certain intense experiences whose significance defied analysis but which were peculiarly one's own."[21] I do not mean to praise Wordsworth because he is like us. But the fact that we share with him certain notions about the dignity and validity of private experience—notions of which *The Prelude* is a very early literary expression—is an interesting fact of cultural history.

The value that both Wordsworth and Mill put on their periods of despondency and mental crisis is important for the same reasons. It connects them with other men of their century. And, again, it connects them with us. However thoroughly we may have cheapened and vulgarized the idea, we still believe, in some very general sense, that to be really serious people we must be "twice-born"—through psychoanalysis, perhaps, or neurotic collapse, or some other deep personal distress. This fact lends urgency to an inquiry into the origins of the notion. Sometimes it seems to have some relation to the experience of religious conversion. Of such experience Carlyle wrote that it marked a man's passage into "spiritual majority." The invention, so to speak, of this experience was to him a great fact of modern history. "It was a new-attained progress in the Moral Development of man: hereby has the Highest come home to the bosoms of the most

Limited; what to Plato was but a hallucination, and to Socrates a chimera, is now clear and certain to your Zinzendorfs, your Wesleys, and the poorest of their Pietists and Methodists."[22] Of those Methodists and the rest and of the autobiographies they wrote, other chapters will speak.

And speak to a particular point. The accounts of themselves that eighteenth-century religious autobiographers give foreshadow the autobiographies of Wordsworth and Mill. The ambiguous relationship between inner and outer life, sometimes issuing in an outright opposition between self and society, has been a principal preoccupation of post-eighteenth-century minds. I suggest that this preoccupation was innocently prepared for by the lives and writings of men who had scarcely a notion of how potently subversive were the value and meaning they discovered in pain.

But, first, what of the normal view of life as it is expressed in autobiographies marked, not by their revelations, but by their reticences? Such works have excellences of their own. Who is to say that Mill's *Autobiography* commands our interest more firmly, more directly, than Gibbon's *Memoirs?* And the fact that a Roger North and a Gibbon make little of purely subjective experiences does not mean that they never underwent any or that such experiences were not important to the formation of their characters. Indeed, I shall suggest of Gibbon that he reclaims for serious attention the large part that loneliness, pain, and illness may play in the development of a consciousness chiefly intellectual. (Like the religious, he transcends his experience of these things; but the transcendence occurs in the world of deeds, not the world of spirit.) And Roger North makes much of the notion that a man is to be known in the privacies of his life, that there his self really resides.

But the moral posture of a North or a Gibbon is finally very different from that of a Wordsworth or a Mill, a Bunyan, a Fox, or a Cowper. From the pages of North and Gibbon we derive on the one hand a sense of a personal rigidity, hard won and heroically maintained, and on the other hand a willingness to trust more or less unquestioningly in received assumptions about reality, a reality which, however hostile it may from time to time have seemed to them, they (unlike the religious autobiographers) conceive to be incapable of revision or displacement by the private consciousness. Reality, in what I here call the normal vision of it, is something one derives certainty about through consensus, not revelation.

II

THE NORMAL VISION

Roger North: A Brother's Life

To say that Roger North's autobiography* expresses the normal view of life is not to say that it is commonplace or boring, for North is seldom dull. It is simply to suggest that, unlike such otherwise disparate persons as Boswell, Bunyan, and even Gibbon, Roger North does not conceive of his life as an object of contemplation. It is not for him a *thing*, an entity to be shaped, re-formed, or even understood; there is no hint that it ever occurred to Roger North that his life had any significance beyond itself. His life is not, in his conception of it, to be conned for a meaning; there is no large lesson in it, for himself or others; no pattern is expected to emerge from his self-scrutiny.

North was a lawyer, and his autobiography is, in outline at least, about what one would expect of an intelligent but not deeply introspective lawyer nowadays. It contains a few pages on his childhood, a few more on his education. He writes about his

* *The Autobiography of the Hon. Roger North*, ed. Augustus Jessop (London, 1887). The manuscript in the British Museum (Add. MS 32, 506) is entitled *Notes of Mee*, the term I shall employ in my text, though citations are to Jessop's edition. The manuscript, a microfilm of which I have examined, displays no great differences from the printed text nor any interesting minor ones.

hobbies and diversions—music, amateur architectural studies, dabblings in science, yachting. And, of course, he tells a good deal about his professional career. He recounts his important cases and his promotions; he includes anecdotes and sketches, friendly and unfriendly, of his colleagues at the bar and the notable judges before whom he has practiced. The book does not really end; North simply trails off into silence, as might any man in like circumstances, his public career over and the uncertain pleasures of retirement facing him. In short, for North as for many, life is simply something one has lived, not a puzzle to be solved or a dark continent to be explored. Life is full of difficulties, yes; but it is not itself a Difficulty. For him it is not quite that interesting.

One does not expect, on the face of it, an autobiography issuing from such a consciousness to have many claims to attention. Historical interest, perhaps; North lived at an interesting time. One brother, Francis, with whom for years he spent much time daily, was Keeper of the Great Seal under Charles II and James II; another brother, Dudley, was a prosperous merchant, a customs official, and a sheriff of London; a third brother, John, was Master of Trinity College, Cambridge; and Roger himself was Temporal Steward to the See of Canterbury, Solicitor General to the Duke of York, and Attorney General to James II's queen. Always, Roger says, he "valued the opportunities" that "living so high upon the rising ground" gave him for joining "a general prospect of human actions . . . with the conversation of the most subtle and prudent men of the age." [1] North's autobiography is chiefly valuable, then, one imagines, as a history of his own times. But this is not entirely so.

For one thing, he does not absolutely ignore the inner life. One way or another, he pays a good deal of attention to his states of mind. At boarding school, he says, for instance: "I began . . . to have a sense of myself." [2] He means exactly what a more self-conscious autobiographer would mean: that he began to be aware that he was different from his companions, a distinct individual with peculiar abilities and weaknesses—a unique and therefore lonely self. Usually, however, he is less explicit and rather more artful. The fact is that North's style and narrative method attain some of the ends of poetry. That is to say, he manages to render a person or occasion so vividly that we seem to experience it as he did and thereby come to know, without his telling us in so many words, what it felt like to be Roger North. He does not name his emotions, but makes us feel them. Thus, of a girl he admired and of her father's treatment of her, he writes: "Here she stayed till her father, like a beast, took her away, to be buried with him alive in the country; where, by the tyranny of his temper, being always cross and perverse, especially to his children, he had broke her to the greatest degree of submission and obedience that I ever observed." [3] North's anger, even years after the event, is fresh. It expresses itself in the simile and metaphor of the first half of the sentence and in that phrase "especially to his children" in the second half, which damns by noting with savage objectivity the *differentia* of this particular cruel man.

Roger North's manner, then, accounts for much of the interest of his work. His eye and his language cooperate to find in the world and memory the data that re-create the past as it appeared to him. Consideration of his manner brings up the question of the relationship of his autobiography to his other, better-known works, the biographies of his three brothers.* The fact is that in no writer, not even Boswell, are the connections between autobiography and biography closer or more interesting. Boswell's *Life of Johnson* consists in considerable part of portions of his autobiographical writings detached from the main body and

* Roger North, *The Lives of the Right Hon. Francis North, Baron Guilford, the Hon. Sir Dudley North, and the Hon. and Rev. Dr. John North* (3 vols.; London, 1836)—hereafter cited as *Lives*.

revised, rearranged, and collated with information from other sources; as a result, the *Life* is really a biography of Johnson, not simply the account of Boswell's friendship with him. Not so with Roger North. Each of his biographies focuses on one of the brothers; but the rest appear in each, in however minor a role. Moreover, almost everything recorded of them is drawn from Roger's memory;* in short, it is part of his own life.

Roger's autobiography consists, we may say, not only of the manuscript modestly entitled *Notes of Mee*, but also of his biographies of his brothers. Roger North's *Lives* and his autobiography are really one work. From that work will emerge eventually Roger North's view of what he himself is first of all—a member of a family. It is a view that Gibbon and Boswell share, though they express it differently and though it has different values for them. For the moment, the point that follows from the kinship among Roger North's essays in life-writing is that North's critical observations on the art of biography apply to his autobiographical practice as consistently as to their ostensible subject.

These critical observations occur here and there throughout the books with which we are concerned and in a remarkable series of paragraphs, probably composed in the second or third decade of the eighteenth century, intended to stand as a preface to the *Lives* but discovered and the most interesting extracts of it published only very recently.[4] The end of life-writing, says North, is instruction. "What signifies it to us, how many battles Alexander fought? It were more to the purpose to say how often he was drunk, and then we might from the ill consequences to him incline to be sober." [5] Here, of course, North is quite conventional. But the instruction life-writing provides, in North's conception of it, is not exactly, or not principally, moral. North

* Letters and other documents, to be sure, are interlarded—sometimes at tedious length.

seems inclined to smile at those who turn to literature for encouragement to virtue. "Works of this kind," he says on the first page of the *Life* of his brother John, "may be useful to such as had rather profit by the example of others, than apply any invention, or industry, of their own, towards a moral improvement; or, it may be, to wear away some heavy hours in reading." [6] He seems to imply that those who read or profess to read for moral instruction are lazy men wasting their time. Is he serious? It is difficult to tell. In any case, the instruction that in the newly discovered preface he proposes as the end of life-writing seems less moral than prudential. Biographies "instruct a private economy," a benefit that is the "gross reason" for writing and reading them; [7] from such works one may garner

> a copious harvest of discretion, and wisdom in common dealing, and disposing the affairs of a family, and making fit provisions for it, and also for the education and settlement of children, and other emergent concerns of human life, to be gathered from the patterns of private men, who have at their great risk proved divers ways of living, and it may be have found out the best at last, and possibly suffered by their mistakes.[8]

Therefore, the "account of a private man's economy, how he was educated, matched, governed his family, conducted his affairs, or passed his time" is a worthy enterprise.[9]

I emphasize North's notion that life-writing can and should teach prudence because that notion helps to explain an important aspect of North's works, his insistence that the flaws of his subjects be displayed as well as their virtues. North's subjects are flawed, but *only* flawed. Their faults are large enough to teach prudential but not moral lessons. It would have been better, Roger seems to say, had his brother Dudley not kept a Turkish concubine, but not very much better; the main point is that, happily, keeping one damaged neither his health nor his fortune. If moral instruction had been the end North had had in view, his own and his brothers' lives would not have served his turn. They were neither monsters of vice nor heroes; rather, they were intelligent, loyal men, with an eye to the main chance but high principled and honorable. In a worldly way, they were all successes, though in Roger's view two of them, Francis and John, were killed by their success. Their lives, as Roger records them, ask us to observe what men of intelligence and vigorous will can achieve, given an even moderately favorable start and a little good luck along the way and despite their undoubted peculiarities and faults.

In drawing attention to his subjects' blemishes, Roger North was doing what he knew to be an unconventional thing. It was something for which he several times (a little truculently) apologized.

> It is a great mistake for any man to expect that, in historical relations, he should be made a hero, and, like them in romances, be always not only blameless but sovereign. No man is without defects and failings, and can claim perfection in nothing but a good will; and any relation, that represents persons otherwise, is false.[10]

Essentially, then, this insistence on the necessity of portraying a man's failings and errors is in the service of North's notion of the realities of personality, which are best revealed in private behavior. A catalogue of a man's "residences, reflections, doubts, melancholies, confidences, with his arts of governing himself and his possessions" is as interesting as an account of his public acts. Indeed, if

> the history of a life hangs altogether upon great importances, such as concern the church and state, and drops the peculiar economy and private conduct of the person that gives title to the work, it may be a history, and a very good one; but of any thing rather than of that person's life. Some may think designs, of that nature,

> to be, like the plots of Mr. Bays, good only to bring in fine things: but a life should be a picture; which cannot be good, if the peculiar features, whereby the subject is distinguished from all others, are left out. Nay, scars and blemishes, as well as beauties, ought to be expressed; otherwise, it is but an outline filled up with lilies and roses.[11]

Life-writing is portraiture, realistic portraiture.

> I fancy myself a picture-drawer, and aiming to give the same image to a spectator, as I have of the thing itself which I desire should be here represented. As, for instance, a tree, in the picture whereof, the leaves and minor branches, are very small and confused, and give the artist more pain to describe, than the solid trunk and greater branches. But, if these small things were left out, it would make but a sorry picture of a tree.[12]

It is just these details that are the hardest for a writer to come by. "Therefore," North says, "a life-writer in education, conversation, and all commerce of life, ought to be the nearest of any allied to his subject, and not a contingent gatherer. . . ." Sadly, "there is seldom or never any one person that can answer for the whole life, and actions of any man, but however friendly and intimate they were, there is remaining absence, employment, or somewhat that hinders a continual notice of his actions, determinations, and occurrences." Even supposing two such companions to exist, North asks, "do such use to keep pocket books, to use for journal memorandums of each other?" [13] It is remarkable how closely North's requirements for a good life-writer, which he despairs of seeing fulfilled, anticipate Boswell's qualifications. Still, even Boswell does not fulfill them entirely; "absence, employment, or somewhat" hindered his "continual notice." The fact is that Roger North's requirements of the good life-writer are so high that they can be met only by the subject himself; the only perfect life, by North's standards, is an autobiography.

For North, then, all life-writing was, if not autobiography, at least autobiographical. To repeat, the essence of good biography for North is detail, private detail, detail observed first hand. It is part of the author's experience, part of his life. It would be wrong to suggest, however, that such detail is the staple of his work. The public and professional lives of his brothers (John excepted) and himself are, if we count the pages devoted to them, much more prominent in these works. For example, he conceives of the life of his brother Francis as punctuated by four momentous events in his public career, and it is around these events, these stages in his brother's progress, that he organizes his biography of him.[14] But what is noteworthy is his insistence, uncommon before his time, that intimate details have any place at all in a "life." The usual attitude toward such matters is well exemplified by John Toland, one of Milton's early biographers. "That a Man, for example, was sick at such a time," Toland wrote, "or well at another, should never be mentioned; except in the Causes or Effects, Cure or Continuance, there happens something remarkable, and for the benefit of Mankind to know." [15] Unless the phrase "benefit of Mankind" be interpreted very broadly, much of the detail North includes would be excluded by a Toland. North again is closer to Boswell, who was confident that "minute particulars are frequently characteristic, and always amusing, when they relate to a distinguished man." [16]

At one point in his *Life* of Dudley, North says:

> But now we have our merchant, sheriff, alderman, commissioner, &c at home with us, a private person, divested of all his mantlings; and we may converse freely with him in his family, and by himself, without clashing at all against any concern of the public. And possibly, in this capacity, I may show the best side of his character.[17]

In these two sentences, we find Roger North preparing to carry into practice the theory of life-writing that he has developed. And there is something else to notice here. That is the tone of these sentences, especially the first one. As the tense implies, his brother in his private life is present to Roger's memory in a way that in his public employments he is not. The best, the real Dudley is only to be discerned when the trappings of office have been put off. Roger delights to have his brother to himself. Indeed, he delighted in the company of all three of the brothers about whom he wrote, and this pleasure lends emotional urgency to his prescriptions for the proper life-writer, for the unstated qualification of such an author is that he love his subject.

Roger North was a lawyer, and in *Notes of Mee* he writes like one, at least for much of his book. But, if all his life-writings are taken together, his biographical autobiography (so to speak) is not that of a lawyer, but of a brother, for this was Roger's true calling. He was not the great lawyer his brother Francis seems to have been; he owed what success he had largely to that brother's influence. But his success at being a brother was entirely his own; it might be said that he had a genius for it. He survived all three, and to him fell the brotherly office of looking after the children two of them left—a duty he performed well and willingly. The very act of composing the *Lives* is evidence of his affection for them, for it expresses his unwillingness to let them die the final death of falling out of all human memory. "For the very remembrance of these things is delight," he says, speaking of his pleasure in music, "and while I write methinks I play." [18] Writing his brothers' *Lives* seems to have given him a similar comfort by bringing them directly before him once again.

It may even be that an explanation for the lateness of his marriage (it did not occur until 1696) is that, while they lived, his brothers were society enough for him. This was most markedly true of his relationship with the oldest of the three, Francis: "he had scarcely a retired minute without me." [19] They took the air together in Francis' coach; they rode together to court. And, when Francis dined out, "unless with grandees of one sort or other," Roger always accompanied him.[20] At dinner at home, when there was company, Roger was often "set at the head of his table, for want of a lady, to carve"; and afterward he poured the tea.[21] To avoid embarrassment at having to take part in the company's "talk (too wise for me)," he would diffidently withdraw and in the next room play upon his viol, a music "which did not (being soft) offend them."[22] At length, when the guests left, Roger would see his brother to bed. Commonly Francis "would unbend himself with a song to my thorough bass before he went into his chamber";[23] there was a harpsichord, too, which stood at Francis' bedroom door and which Roger "touched to his voice."[24]

The portrait of Francis that emerges from this is not an altogether pleasant one. "And, to say truth," Roger interjects at one point,

> I . . . could scarce brook the many mortifications, by little contempts my brother, sometimes in jest and often in earnest, would put upon me. He had somewhat of a humour that way of raising his own by depressing others' characters.

At length Roger "broke out in resentment," saying that he "had endured patiently for ten years"; and from then on Francis was "tender" of Roger's pride.* But Francis is always his "best

* *Autobiography of Roger North*, p. 91. It may be that even these unpleasant details do not tell the whole story. A comparison of the manuscript of the *Lives* (B.M. Add. MS 32, 508) with the printed text reveals that Roger (or his son, who first edited it) at last suppressed certain anecdotes showing Francis in a bad light. One that illustrates his cruel wit concerns his days at college. Francis "with his little Eyes observed every Body, & used to gather remarks for his own, all the vain and Rediculous actions of those, who in that way fell obnoxious to him: and then made the fellows merry with his Relating them; & they, for their diversion, encouraged him; and he never failed to Seis upon every foolish Behaviour, & described it, not in the satirical, but in such veritable manner, as if the thing had been seen, as well as told." Quoted by James L. Clifford in "Roger North and the Art of Biography," in *Restoration and Eighteenth Century Literature*, ed. Carroll Camden (Chicago, 1963), p. 280.

brother"—he uses the phrase repeatedly—and Roger was "a shadow to him, as if they had grown together." [25] Francis, for all his inclination to use and condescend to Roger, "never was so well, as when any of his family relations, whom he was continually obliging, were with him." [26]

Of the relationship between Francis and Dudley, the energetic Turkey merchant, Roger says that "each was an Indies to the other, producing always the richest novelties, of which the best understandings are greedy." [27] John, too, the young and eccentric Master of Trinity, was "whole-footed" only "when some of his nearest relations were with him." [28] Then John

> loved to spar questions, and foment disputes, and then whip into the chair as moderator; and they must . . . make good their arguments, or let go their hold. . . . And, in this manner, the doctor and his near friends, with utmost content and satisfaction, used to entertain their hours, when affairs permitted them to be so happy.[29]

"Near friends"—the phrase is interesting. North frequently uses that term for his brothers, and it suggests, I think, the nature of the relationship among them. Brothers need not be friends. Indeed, Charles, the oldest of the Norths of that generation and the heir to the family title, was *not* a friend (and Roger did not write his life). He was "not contented that any of our common concerns should pass quietly and smooth," says Roger delicately of the trouble he made over the settlement of their mother's estate.[30] But the others were the closest of friends. And they were friends, too, in a sense of the word that has rather passed out of use—that of composing a party, in the sense of, say, "the King's friends," by which is implied not congeniality so much as common loyalty and common interest.

There were several reasons for this, of which the first was political. Public men in the age of Charles II and James II, Titus

Oates and the rest had great need of friends in this sense of the term, men whom they could trust absolutely, or at all. These brothers performed this office for one another. It was a litigious age as well. Roger mentions it as a remarkable circumstance that Dudley was sued only once in his life.[31] Even members of different generations of the same family might go to law with one another. For instance, the Norths' father was suspicious of Francis' offer to help him draw his will.[32] The grandfather, too, was far from trusting. Once, thinking to trap Francis, he commanded him to produce some legal papers, the drawing of which he had paid for but which he did not believe his grandson to have performed. When, to his surprise, Francis in fact produced the papers and asked what he should do with them,

> the old lord, being utterly frustrated in his expectations, turned about the room quicker than ordinary; and as he mended his pace, Frank was in great doubt what was to become of him. At last he ventured to say, "My lord, what is your pleasure I shall do with these papers?" The old lord stopped short, and turning, said, "wipe your —— with them." That answer was not at all expected. . . .[33]

But these are negative reasons for the league that the brothers formed. Safety was not their only concern. The help they could afford one another in the forwarding of their fortunes was a stronger motive. Francis, the most successful on his own account, was of course the most powerful of them—the "sheet anchor," Roger calls him at one point. Perhaps we should imagine him as president of a family firm, for so he appears in this summary passage at the end of Roger's biography of him.

> I have here showed how a half-decayed family, with a numerous brood, and worn-out estate, of the Norths, by the auspicious character of one child of ten, was re-edified; and all the rest lifted into the world with wonderful success; and no one of the whole pack miscarried, or were not in all respects (the eldest excepted) mutu-

> ally helpful and assistant to each other; and none of them tainted with any vice or dishonour, nor the least favour of difference, or feud, found amongst them; but, from the first to the last, they maintained their fraternal amity and correspondence inviolable. I say (not derogating from the influences of a virtuous parentele) most of all these felicities were derived from the patronage of his lordship. . . .[34]

Under their eccentric, uneconomical, and long-lived grandfather, Dudley, Third Baron North (1581–1666), the fortunes of the family had declined sharply. It was the business of Roger's generation to re-establish the Norths in a position of wealth and power. This they had to combine to do, and combine they did, in that league of "fraternal amity" under Francis their chief.

In this project of theirs, they were largely successful, as the list of their accomplishments in the law, politics, trade, and the university makes clear. But the three whom Roger loved best died relatively young, and, with the accession of William and Mary, Roger, himself loyal to the Stuarts, abandoned hope of further preferment. It is at this point that *Notes of Mee* ends—as though with the death of his brothers and the dissolution of their "corporation" Roger's best life were over. For, as I have said, his calling was to be a brother. His intercourse with his brothers provides the most interesting of his experiences. *Notes of Mee*, to be sure, makes something of his life on his own. Rather touchingly, he devotes five of the not very numerous pages of that book to one minor but happy occasion, an excursion of several days on his yacht. The day of his departure

> proved cool, the gale brisk, air clear, and no inconvenience to molest us, nor wants to trouble our thoughts, neither business to importune, nor formalities to tease us; so that we came nearer to perfection of life there than I was ever sensible otherwise. . . . And at midnight, in the air, the eating cold meat and bread, and drinking small beer, was a regale beyond imagination. I can say,

> I scarce ever knew the pleasure of eating till then, and have not observed the like on any occasion since.[35]

There is something a little pathetic about a life that provides no greater delights than these, substantial though they are, or provides them only once. But Roger's life seems not really to have been pathetic, and his brothers were the reason.

He took Dudley out on that yacht, for instance; immediately

> he claps himself down upon the seat by the helm, and, taking the whipstaff in his hand, "By G—," said he, "I'll be admiral"; and there he sat, and steered, with all the delight imaginable. And no entertainment pleased him better than this; because he sat all the while; and, besides acting and conduct, which to him was always relishing, he could look about and talk; which was bringing into his time as much of what he loved as was possible.[36]

Roger's pleasure in this occasion is unmistakable, as are the amusement and love with which he beholds his vivid brother.

Dudley, rather more attractive than the patronizing Francis, became a great companion of Roger's. His unexpected arrival in London after years in the Mediterranean makes a remarkable scene. Appearing on Francis' doorstep at eight in the morning, he is greeted by an old servant he had known as a boy, a woman so "pthisical" that she "could scarce crawl up stairs once a day."

> This gentleman appearing with his mustachios, according to the Turkish manner, *Cordubee* hat, and strange out-of-the-way clothes, just as if one had been dressed up to act Captain Dangerfield in the play, she stood staring at him; and he, knowing her, called her by name. By that she knew it was her Master Dudley, and flew up stairs to tell the news, as if she had been a girl of sixteen. . . . After a quarter of an hour's conversation, we sent him to a chamber to refresh, whilst we got up. . . . His first demand was a tailor, a tailor. The tailor came, but could not finish

> his office, in civilizing a *barbare*, under two days; and all that time he wore his Dangerfield habit and beard. It was pleasant to see him manage his mustachios; for, being apt to trespass upon the mouth, they were always, by an action, habitually put by, before drinking, one way and the other. But yet the beard would have a share out of the glass, and was made clean again by another habitual action of sipping the upper lip.[37]

Only with difficulty did Dudley translate himself back into English. After he had shaved,

> it was considerable time before his upper lip . . . took the same tawn as the rest of his face; but, looking white and pale, made a strange disfigurement. And it was a matter of ridicule to see him always, before drinking, act with his fingers to part away his (then) no beard; and, when he had done, to sip his upper lip, although the mop, to be cleaned, was gone.[38]

These are incidents in the biography of Dudley; but just as clearly they are part of Roger's autobiography. The facts are facts of Dudley's life, but the observation of them is a fact of Roger's. Utterances of Dudley's incorporated into the biography because they help to characterize him may be equally important for an understanding of Roger. Thus when Roger reports that Dudley, to quell his own spirit when it rebelled at frustration, used to exclaim: "The Pope hath not his will, the king of France hath not his will, the king of England hath not his will, the devil hath not his will, and by G— I will not have my will," [39] we learn something, surely, about Roger, if it is only that he finds the same sort of thing amusing that we do. The sweetness of Roger's description of Dudley's married life communicates a sense of his notion of what domestic happiness is. Dudley had married for love, and Roger had played a part in the business negotiations that preceded the match. The bride's father was not pleased with

Dudley and indeed did not become reconciled to him until the shrewd Dudley, newly chosen sheriff of London, tempted him with the panoply of his office. "Come, son, let us go out and shine," the old man used to say.[40] After the wedding, the couple took a large house in London—so large that Dudley used one of the principal rooms to make vinegar in. At home, Dudley was seldom absent from his wife's side; in a little dressing room "she had her implements, and he his books of account," and together they worked. "If time lay on his hands, he would assist his lady in her affairs. I have come there and found him very busy in picking out the stitches of a dislaced petticoat." [41] When their children were sick, Dudley nursed them; and often he dressed them or put them to bed at night. The biographer of a modern husband would scarcely note such details; they are too commonplace. The interest here is that such behavior in a husband was unusual, and the charm is that it was voluntary. The affection it expressed, his tone suggests, Roger admired and perhaps envied.

At Francis' death, Dudley and Roger became the trustees of his heir, and, in the discharge of that office, they passed part of the summers at Wroxton, the house that the young lord had inherited, overseeing the management of the place. To entertain themselves, they set up a "manufactory" in one of the outbuildings, a combination of a carpenter's and a blacksmith's shop. Dudley preferred carpentry. "He allowed me, being a lawyer, as he said, to be the best forger." [42] Their activities and their costume—Dudley usually appeared in "a red short waistcoat, red cap, and black face"—mystified the country people; even Dudley's wife was "full of admiration what creatures she had in her family." [43] Between them they devised a "waywiser," or odometer, a fantastic contraption of wheels within wheels which they called "Sir Theophilus Gimcrack" and which they dragged about the countryside in a chaise, measuring distances and entertaining themselves by comparing their results with "the unaccountable variety of vulgar estimates." [44]

The vividness of this passage in Dudley's biography is owing to its being a passage in Roger's as well. And something else is suggested here—the interest that all the brothers, and Roger not the least, had in experiments in mechanics, architecture, and engineering. One value of Roger's books is that they document our notions about the vigor of the scientific spirit among amateurs in the seventeenth century. Francis, it seems, was invited to join the Royal Society, but turned the offer down.[45] All the brothers had scientific interests that might have qualified them for membership. Even John, a clergyman and a Platonist, kept "great house spiders in wide-mouthed glasses, such as men keep tobacco in." He fed them flies and observed carefully how the spiders trapped and ate them—and one another. "The doctor used to divert us with describing the course of life which his poor prisoners led." [46]

On Saturdays, Dudley and Roger used to stop by St. Paul's, then being built, and question Sir Christopher Wren, "who, like a true philosopher, was always obliging and communicative, and, in every matter we inquired about, gave short, but satisfactory answers." [47] Both the brothers were passionate architects. "He drew, and I drew, and much altercation we had," Roger says cheerfully.[48] Roger had considerable experience in architectural drawing, beginning with the plan he drew for his own chambers in the rebuilt Inner Temple, and he delighted in depicting buildings "in their nudities." [49] Mathematics, too, interested him. At college he had studied geometry under his brother John's tutelage; at first it had seemed dull, but at last a certain proposition "entered me alive," and his interest in the study survived the years.[50] Even sailing, when he took that up, he considered one of his "mathematical entertainments," because it was a "mechanical" art.[51] As a law student, Roger had amused himself by designing what he thought was a perpetual-motion machine, a project from which he was discouraged by Francis, "who had been sick of the same infirmity." [52] But he prosecuted his studies in mechanics to the point where he thought that he could explain windmills, ships making way to windward, "and other exotic forces" better than other students of these matters.[53] In *Notes of Mee*, he offhandedly offers a "physical solution" to "Mr. Newton's hypothesis" about light, a theory he "ever admired . . . as new and most exquisitely thought." [54]

What is striking here is the confidence of this amateur; it is misplaced confidence, of course, for his "solution" is worthless. But, to such intelligent gentlemen as the Norths, it did not seem odd to quiz the greatest architect of the age or to venture to supplement the speculations of Newton. And the Norths' interest in these serious matters is of a piece with the fun they had with Sir Theophilus Gimcrack and their fascination with the "knick-knack-atory" of a Mr. Weld who mysteriously "sowed sallads in the morning, to be cut for dinner" and "claimed the invention of painted curtains in varnish upon silk, which would bend and not crack." [55] They seriously debated with Sir Samuel Moreland "the grand affair of the mercurial barometer" at the same time as they wondered admiringly at the devices of which that gentleman's house was full, among them "a portable engine, that moved by watchwork, which might be called a kitchen; for it had a fireplace and grate, with which he could make a soup, broil costellets, or roast an egg." [56]

The Norths' confidence in the face of the complexity of nature, their easy equation of tinkering with invention and experiment, is impossible now for men of their intelligence. But, in their own day, they seem not to have been so very extraordinary. It was not in spite of his amateur spirit that Francis was invited to join the Royal Society, but partly because of it. That society, according to Thomas Sprat, proposed

> a *Philosophy* for the use of *Cities*, and not for the retirement of *Schools*, to resemble the *Cities* themselves: which are compounded

> of all sorts of men, of the *Gown*, of the *Sword*, of the *Shop*, of the *Field*, of the *Court*, of the *Sea;* all mutually assisting each other.[57]

The Norths were themselves a miniature society of this sort, and perhaps that is part of the reason Francis declined membership. In any event, the apparent confidence of the Society and of the Norths that any intelligent person can arrive at the truths of nature seems to issue from a certainty that the world contains no mysteries, only secrets—an attitude consonant with the notion that, for Roger North, life, though full of problems, is not itself a Problem.

Roger was, in his time, a very modern man. His most ambitious intellectual project was the construction of "a system of nature, upon the Cartesian or rather mechanical principles," for he believed that "all the common phenomena of nature might be resolved into them." [58] Though he never completed this project, the very conception of it marks him as a man of advanced ideas. But Roger's sensibilities were attuned to what was old in England as well as to what was new. One virtue of Roger's account of his life is its occasional evocation of a valuable vanished past. The circumstances of his life had encouraged in him a sense of how in even a few years a world could change, and not for the better. For Roger was still in his thirties when his best-loved brothers were dead and his public career at an end.

The revolution of 1688 marked an era in his life. "I do not swear," writes Roger of his political position,[59] and the phrase explains his retirement to country pleasures and meditation upon the past. His childhood is, as we might expect, one of the lost worlds of which he speaks; and it is lost not only because he is no longer a child, but because such things as "the now-reigning humour of running to London" have made old customs, old manners fall into disuse.[60] Recalling his grandfather's love of music,

Roger writes that this "retired old fantastic courtier" took a fancy to a wood a mile or so from his house and "cut glades and made arbours in it, and no name would fit the place but Tempe. Here he would convoke his musical family, and songs were made and set for celebrating the joys there, which were performed, and provisions carried up." [61] To this pastoral perfection, Roger contrasts things as they are now, when a musician must be an expert or not play at all, so that country families feel ashamed of innocently entertaining themselves as the Norths did. Here, obviously enough, is Roger's amateurism again; it is supplemented by his observation of the superior pleasure the performer has in comparison to the audience. "So if a nail is to be driven," he remarks acutely, "and two or three stand by, each has a mind and would be pleased to do it." [62] As usual in reminiscence, the balance between past and present favors the former. What has been lost is pleasure and simplicity, and the loss constitutes a diminution of virtue.

Roger's account of his earliest schooling, in the family of a local clergyman, Ezekiel Catchpole, bears a similar charge. In Roger's portrait of him, this man resembles Chaucer's Parson or Fielding's Abraham Adams: "the parson himself and his son wrought hard in harvest, and none was so inconsiderable as to stand out; in short, it was a direct farmer's economy." [63] Roger's practical education, he acknowledges, owed something to his informal exposure to this "economy," as his moral education owed something to Catchpole's example. Though the parson was "very penurious," says Roger,

> yet the loaf, and small beer were always free to his family to come to, . . . and never was any poor man whatever that asked an alms by right-down begging, or with fiddle or pipe as often is done, who went away without relief of that sort, and broken meat when there was any, but that was seldom.

Such he holds to be a reproach to "the opulent clergy, who puff their housekeeping." [64] At that time, the parish itself consisted of small farms and dairies,

> so that business was usually done by noon, and it was always the custom of the youth of the town, who were men or maid servants, and children, to assemble, after horses baited, either upon the green or (after haysel) in a close accustomed to be so used, and there all to play till milking time, and supper at night. The men to football, and the maids, with whom we children commonly mixed, being not proof for the turbulence of the other party, to stoolball, and such running games as they knew. And all without mixing men and women, as in dancing with the fiddle, but apart. No idle or lascivious frolics between them, and at last all parting to their stations.[65]

In kind, these evocations of the past are grandfather stories, the staple of memoir and reminiscence in which old gentlemen discourse at tedious length on the superiority to the present of some past that the reader or listener guesses never quite existed. We may wonder whether there were *never* any "idle or lascivious frolics between" Roger's companions, any heavy labor and suffering. But Roger North's memories have a charm that many lack. One notices the ease and particularity of the style here. The kinds of beggars and the kinds of food are specified, and the games and who played them, and where and when. These details express the clarity and, by implication, the high value of this early recollection to Roger. He is not merely bewailing the passing of a virtuous world. He is holding it in memory and offering it to his readers as a re-created thing, a moral landscape, so to speak, to which we may compare the present, not for the purpose of rejecting and turning our faces away from that present, but to the end of revising it in the light of the ideal of possibility that the past represents.

Nowhere is this clearer than in Roger's description of the

"princely oeconomy" of Badminton, the house of the Duke of Beaufort near Bristol where he and Francis once passed a week. The place and the duke's manner of living there were for Roger the pattern of magnificence and graciousness, a model for gentlemen to imitate. The house itself was nobly planned and landscaped—always an important consideration to the Norths. It stood at the center of an "asterisk of glades cut through the wood of all the country round, four or five in a quarter." [66] The household numbered about two hundred, all under good discipline, a circumstance which, to judge from Roger's wonder at it, was rare in those great houses. No necessary expense was spared. At the entrance to his estate, for example, the duke had built, solely for the convenience of his guests, "pompous stables" which could shelter forty horses. (One advantage of this was that a visitor's servant could care for his master's horse instead of turning it over to one of the duke's grooms, who would expect a large tip.) But there was no "vain ostentation" of wealth. The family did not hesitate to spend money, but nothing was bought that could be made at home, be it malt, candles, or bedding.[67] The manner of life of the masters of Badminton, like their management of their affairs, united relative simplicity with a candid enjoyment of their blessings.

> As for the duke and duchess, and their friends, there was no time of day without diversion. Breakfast in her gallery that opened into the gardens; then, perhaps a deer was to be killed, or the gardens, and parks with the several sorts of deer, to be visited; and if it required mounting, horses of the duke's were brought for all the company. And so, in the afternoon, when the ladies were disposed to air, and the gentlemen with them, coaches and six came to hold them all. At half an hour after eleven the bell rang to prayers, so at six in the evening: and, through a gallery, the best company went into an aisle in the church (so near it was), and the duke and duchess could see if all the family were

> there. The ordinary pastime of the ladies was in a gallery on the other side, where she had divers gentlewomen commonly at work upon embroidery and fringemaking; for all the beds of state were made and finished in the house. The meats were very neat, and not gross; no servants in livery attended, but those called gentlemen only; and in the several kinds, even down to the small beer, nothing could be more choice than the table was. It was an oblong, and not an oval; and the duchess, with two daughters only, sat at the upper end. If the gentlemen chose a glass of wine, the civil offers were made either to go down into the vaults, which were very large and sumptuous, or servants, at a sign given, attended with salvers, &c and many a brisk round went about; but no sitting at a table with tobacco and healths, as the too common use is.[68]

All was "incomparable variety," says Roger,

> for the duke had always some new project of building, walling, or planting, which he would show, and ask his friends their advice about it; and nothing was forced, or strained, but easy and familiar, as if it was, and really so I thought it to be, the common course and way of living in that family.[69]

There is something almost wistful in these last words of Roger's. To take a low view of the matter, he is flattered by these attentions from the great. But that fact is not sufficient to explain the tone that Roger takes in this passage. The manner of life at Badminton, its style, its decorum are what the Norths are bent on achieving for themselves. Their own family had once lived in rather this fashion, though not on so grand a scale; it was a return to magnificence that the brothers were trying to accomplish. And this passage makes clear that the Norths' desire was not simply for luxury and power. The great house of Badminton exercises, at least for Roger, a moral attraction. It is the emblem of a condition of life to which he aspires, a setting that expresses the magnanimous man who is its master. This notion of a house as representing a moral idea is, in one sense, conventional enough;

witness Marvell in his poem "Upon Appleton House" and, later, Pope in his *Moral Essays*. But the very fact that Roger North does not explicitly make the point of Badminton's meaning to him suggests, I think, how deeply rooted, how nearly instinctive such a response could be for a man of his time; it went without saying.

Badminton is, then, an ideal of economy, representing in both a financial and an aesthetic sense the perfect adjustment of means to ends; it is an ideal of order in the sense of a harmonious relationship between host and guest, master and man. Badminton may still exist at the time Roger is writing, but it is past for him; he no longer visits there. And it is past because it stands for those values of life that in Roger's view have been subverted by the revolution of 1688. In this, it is one with his grandfather's Tempe and the village sports of his childhood.

It is interesting to speculate on the connections between such imputations as Roger's of special virtue to a past and an interest in life-writing. Autobiography and that species of biography that Roger North practiced are first of all exercises in recollection—recollection in its simplest conception, as the tactic the mind employs to mitigate the destructive powers of time. What lasts need not be remembered; it is transience against which we wage war. And hence it is not surprising that, in the seventeenth century, life-writing, the art of memory, began to flourish, for that century, carrying out the implications of the one that preceded it, was one of the first in which a thoroughgoing revision of the forms of thought and the institutions of social, political, and religious life occurred so quickly as to constitute for each reflective witness a transformation of the world. Roger North expresses in his idealizations of the past his awareness of that transformation, and he deplores it. As the centuries pass, life-writers —and autobiographers especially—internalize and individualize this notion of a vanished past to the point that a time in private rather than in public history stands in judgment on the present, either as a prison from which the writer has escaped or as a paradise from which he has been expelled. But, no matter how that past is conceived, life-writing expresses the prominence in consciousness of change as a primary fact of life.

Perhaps this sense of the precarious existence of things has something to do with another element in Roger North's autobiographical writings—his portraits of interesting contemporaries. His official motive for making these sketches so prominent is that they tell much about his brothers and himself. As Roger does not resist remarking, "A man is known by the company he keeps." [70] In practice, however, Roger's interest goes deeper than this.

Among the most memorable of the characters he preserves is Sir Edmund Saunders, who rose by his own charm and merit from illiterate obscurity to be chief justice of the King's Bench. Even after he became successful, this cheerful bachelor lived at the house of a tailor whose wife was "his nurse, or worse." Saunders drank too much, and his figure showed it:

> he was very corpulent and beastly; a mere lump of morbid flesh. He used to say, "by his troggs," (such a humourous way of talking he affected) "none could say he wanted issue of his body, for he had nine on his back." He was a fetid mass, that offended his neighbours at the bar in the sharpest degree. Those, whose ill fortune it was to stand near him, were confessors, and, in summertime, almost martyrs.[71]

Yet he was popular with his colleagues; when one "grumbled at the stench, he ever converted the complaint into content and laughing with the abundance of his wit." And he was

> a very Silenus to the boys. . . . I have seen him, for hours and half-hours together, before the court sat, stand at the bar, with an audience of students over against him, putting of cases, and debating so as suited their capacities, and encouraged their industry.[72]

Saunders is preserved forever in Roger's lines; but the portrait scarcely serves its ostensible purpose of illuminating Francis' life. Roger is concerned to rescue from oblivion a particular figure and personality, a man of no great note who nevertheless deserves somehow to live on simply because of his oddity. Unlike the ideal pasts Roger records, this portrait bears no positive moral charge. It quietly makes the point that a man's physical aspect may not be the image of his character, that ugliness can consort with virtue. But this observation is not the center of Roger's interest in Saunders. It is Saunders' uniqueness that Roger prizes; his moral worth and meaning are quite secondary to that. Saunders is a phenomenon and deserves to be collected, like information about the oddities of nature. It is the individual and the particular that Roger values, here as in his insistence in his remarks on biography on the importance of private, mean detail. Men's resemblance to one another is observable in every generation. What perishes with a man is what has distinguished him from others. His individuality, his identity, his very self are in every sense of the word his peculiarity.

A slight contradiction may be implicit in all this. Roger's record of certain moments of the past has, we have seen, an ideal cast. He is there resisting the power of time to transform the world. So, too, by treasuring up in writing the characters of his brothers and himself and such men as Saunders, he attempts to withstand the forces of dissolution. He is nostalgic, old fashioned, anecdotal. But, at the same time, his interest in particularities, individual men, oddity, and apparent contradiction expresses the inquisitive, experimental consciousness that he shared with the advanced men of his time; and it was this cast of mind that was at least partly responsible for the changes he deplored. We need not demand of Roger North a philosophical consistency that few in any age can display. Nor need we ingeniously argue him out of his difficulty, if that is what it is. We may speculate about the matter, nevertheless; and one possibility is that Roger North's relationship as a scientist (of however primitive a sort) to his world is not so different from his more fully human relationship to it as is that of the modern scientific mentality. In short, it may be that Roger's interest in what are, in one sense, the data of his investigations survives his learning something about them. Sailing, we remember, was one of his mathematical studies; but he liked sailing for its own sake, too. And so with people. Saunders was a specimen; he was also a delight. Roger not only observes and uses his "facts"; he loves them.

Roger North's autobiography, we have seen, consists not only of *Notes of Mee*, but of all his life-writings. By itself, *Notes of Mee* is a pale performance; but, taken together with his *Lives* of his brothers, it is a fine autobiographical expression of the normal view of life. The fact is that the reader derives from Roger North's life-writings a fuller sense of him than of any of his subjects. We can read any author in his book, but that truth is not sufficient to explain the present case. Roger was a brother. The self his autobiographical writings express is that of a man defined, and his value and function created by his membership in that snug corporation of friends, an affectionate set of brothers. To Boswell and Gibbon, the conception of themselves as part of a family was also important, and it is partly this that sets them off with Roger from the religious autobiographers. (The identity of the religious is less likely to be affected by *any* of his relationships with other people. The overwhelming realities for him are God and himself. Especially among the poor, of course, the dynastic family identifiable from generation to generation, an economic institution that exacts duties and promises rewards, simply does not exist.) But, unlike Roger, Boswell and Gibbon think of their descent from the past, not their companions in the present. Family is for them more abstract: the ancient name and blood of the

Boswells must be preserved and transmitted; the energies of earlier generations of Gibbons, represented by the money they accumulated and managed to hang onto, must express themselves in a great production of art. For Roger, however, his living family, and not even all of that, are his world.

Out of all this arises a sense of some fundamental weakness or timidity in Roger North. He is even less sufficient unto himself than are most of us. To be sure, he did not give in to himself. "I was a plant of slow growth, and when mature but slight wood, and of a flashy fruit," he remarks; still, he resolved to persist "against all my private discouragements, and whatever absurdities and errors I committed in public I would not desist, but forget them as fast as I could, and take more care another time." [73] He ascribes part of his weakness to a "cruel fit of sickness I had when young." [74] But the fact is that he was just not very interested in himself or his own private condition. Reality was *out there* somewhere. Not very *far* out, to be sure; he was content to have the circle of his brothers describe its limits. But the point is that it was not the self, the self in the sense of the inner life, that interested him. For Roger North, the self is defined by its intercourse with persons and things outside; in that intercourse, the individual peculiarities of a man reveal themselves, and these are the *differentia* that the life-writer, whether biographer or autobiographer, cherishes and records. Emphasis on what happens, on how a man behaves—emphasis, in short, on observable phenomena—characterizes what I here call the normal view of life, the view of men who live or think they live in others.

Autobiography so conceived was, I suggest, more capable of telling important truth in Roger North's time than in ours. For, though it seems likely that most men nowadays, if required to write an autobiography, would produce something recognizably akin to Roger North's (his view is still normal in this statistical sense), we would not repose in their works as much confidence as we do in Roger's that it tells the essential truth about the realities of a life. Our notions of what really matters to a man, of what his life feels like to him, have been revised, and we will accept no evidence to the contrary, not even his own.

Gibbon's Fortunes

Whatever Roger North's distinctions, he weighs lightly in the balance with Edward Gibbon. If Gibbon's autobiography as well as North's is taken to express the normal view of life, that normality must be conceived of still less than North's as in any pejorative sense "ordinary." For, obviously, Gibbon was nothing if not extraordinary—in his talents, ambitions, and achievements, on the one hand, and in his figure, his features, and his dress on the other. Even his preferred place of residence was not English. Still, Gibbon's is one of the names that comes naturally and rightly to mind when one attempts to list the Englishmen who dominated the culture of his time. In that sense, his life was normal—brilliantly so.

As usual, Lytton Strachey is almost right:

> Happiness is a word that immediately rises to the mind at the thought of Edward Gibbon: and happiness in its widest connotation—including good fortune as well as enjoyment. Good fortune, indeed, followed him from the cradle to the grave in the most tactful way possible; occasionally it appeared to fail him; but its absence always turned out to be a blessing in disguise.[75]

What is wrong here is the tone. To speak of Gibbon's good fortune as following him "in the most tactful way possible" raises a smile, no doubt; but for the sake of momentary effect it reduces an essentially accurate perception to triviality. For Gibbon's life was not quite as Strachey describes it—a happy, easy progress from joy to joy. Gibbon's own notion of the matter was, at any rate, quite different. It seemed to him that his good fortune consisted less in successes achieved than in disasters avoided.

In a sense, of course, Gibbon's autobiography does not exist or exists as a cooperative venture only very recently completed. The book that for a century and a half has passed for his *Memoirs* is a compilation by his literary executor, John Holroyd, Lord Sheffield, from some six drafts and additional fragments that Gibbon composed between 1788 and 1793. In general, Lord Sheffield's procedure was the only sensible one. Where versions overlapped, he chose the one that treated a given period most fully. Thus, the first third consists largely of version F, written in 1792–1793. The next third consists of version B, and the last is made up of part of version C and much of version E. He did not, however, carry out his own plan mechanically. For instance, he imported into the text from version C the famous "I sighed as a lover; I obeyed as a son," rightly believing it superior to Gibbon's statement of his renunciation of Mlle. Curchod in B, the version he was chiefly following at the moment. There are many such evidences of Lord Sheffield's editorial intelligence. But unfortunately Lord Sheffield's labors did not end here, and when, in the late nineteenth century, the full text of all the versions was published, it became apparent that, well conceived though his edition was, it was incomplete and badly needed revision.[76] In obedience to his notions of propriety, Lord Sheffield had omitted or altered a word here and a passage there, with the result that, however striking still, the book he printed is tamer and less interesting than what Gibbon wrote. Although this fact has been known for almost seventy years, no editor before Dero A. Saunders, whose edition appeared in 1961, attempted to produce a coherent, faithful text of the work.*

* Dero A. Saunders, ed., *The Autobiography of Edward Gibbon* (New York, 1961). Hereafter, citations of this work will appear within parentheses in the text.

Saunders' intention in re-editing the autobiography is, he tells us, to "introduce new readers to the historian, in the hope that they will thereby be led to the history" (p. 24). That hope is probably vain. It has become almost a commonplace to remark, with the great British scholar G. Birkbeck Hill, that, for "one reader who has read his *Decline and Fall*, there are at least a score who have read his autobiography. . . ." [77] As Donald Stauffer puts it: "How many people . . . know how and where Gibbon began and finished the *Decline and Fall of the Roman Empire* who know neither how nor where the Roman Empire fell?" [78] There is good reason for this, and it is not simply the negative one sometimes adduced, that the autobiography is shorter and less demanding than the great history.

Autobiography presents peculiar problems to the critic, for it (more than any other genre) necessarily and incessantly tempts him away from "pure" literary considerations to judgments on the character of the author. Such judgments are, no doubt, finally proper—but *only* finally. In Gibbon's case, especially, if the true nature of his autobiography is to be understood, the critic's moral passions must be indulged with uncommon tact. For the temptation to judge—and judge harshly—is unusually great. Gibbon was not in any ordinary sense an attractive person. His virtues and those of his book are not charming ones. Nevertheless, they are real, and they will be missed by those who concentrate on such easy targets as Gibbon's smugness, vanity, and coldness of heart.

No doubt it is the abundance of those easy targets that makes ordinary opinion about his autobiography so unsatisfactory. The usual critical tactic is to praise the book and deplore the man. Having said that the book is "without a rival," G. Birkbeck Hill can find nothing better to say of its subject than that he had an "original and interesting nature." [79] These carefully noncommittal adjectives we frequently utter when confronted by something surprising, puzzling, and indistinctly minatory. To apply them to Gibbon is appropriate, in a sense; but surely it is not to say the last word. This notion of Gibbon as someone against whom one must defend oneself finds its most direct and vulgar expression in the introduction to the "Everyman" edition. There Oliphant Smeaton contrives to triumph over Gibbon by condescending to praise his "little outcrops of egotism" because they show him to have been "no demi-god, but merely a man of like passions with ourselves"—passions, as it turns out, that are "death to the respect whereon love must be based." [80] Smeaton very neatly has it both ways.

The "Everyman" introduction is inconsequential as criticism, but both Smeaton's and G. Birkbeck Hill's remarks appear to issue from an interesting misconception of the nature of the work with which they are concerned. Both men seem implicitly to conceive of Gibbon's book—and perhaps every autobiography—as an apologia. If it is not, they imply, it *ought* to be. This misunderstanding of the tasks that autobiography may perform, this limitation of its scope, forces them into the contradiction of congratulating Gibbon on his frankness while accusing him of an insufficient sense of shame.

In short, Gibbon's critics have failed or refused to meet him on his own ground. Gibbon seems to have had no notion that his life required defense or, if it did, that it was his place to supply it. To say that Gibbon did not mean to apologize for anything is not, of course, to say that he had nothing to apologize for; but at least it helps us to see what the book is really about. Not apology and self-justification, but "Truth—naked, unblushing truth" is his object (p. 27). Such avowals are conventional enough in the early pages of autobiographies, but Gibbon seems really to have meant what he said. As always, history is on his mind. Gibbon's early ambition to write a biography of Sir Walter Raleigh had been frustrated by the paucity of information about his subject's private life—details that are, he says, "the most essential and important to a biographer" (p. 139). Gibbon himself will someday have a biographer, he knows; it would be false modesty in him to think otherwise, for "the public is always curious to know the men who have left behind them any image of their minds" (p. 30). Therefore he will provide the facts: "I must be conscious that no one is so well qualified as myself to describe the series of my thoughts and actions" (p. 30). The process of setting down that series is amusing, he finds (p. 27), and his "social sympathy," too, is gratified "by the idea that now, in the present hour, he is imparting some degree of amusement or knowledge to his friends in a distant land, that one day his mind will be familiar to the grandchildren of those who are yet unborn" (p. 206).

In all of this, what is new or almost new, at any rate—is the assumption that the thoughts and activities of any man of note are automatically interesting. Gibbon writes his autobiography because the success of the *Decline and Fall* has made him an object of legitimate, morally neutral curiosity. His great history is the occasion of his autobiography and the justification for it.

His autobiography is, then, not so much the life of Edward Gibbon, a private person, as it is the life of the author of the *Decline and Fall*. So much G. Birkbeck Hill admits, when he is not quarreling with Gibbon's faults: "He who had written the *Decline and Fall* had a right to tell the world how he had been prepared for his great task." [81] But Gibbon was doing something more ambitious than exercising a right. As Roy Pascal, a student of autobiography referred to earlier, remarks: "The peculiar significance of his account lies in his inclusion of numerous types of experience that contributed, he recognizes, to his development as a historian." [82] Some of these influences—of books and tutors, for example—we would naturally expect him to record. But others come as something of a surprise. Gibbon recognizes and thereby dignifies and reclaims for serious attention a whole class of experiences—of idleness, illness, lovelessness, isolation—that had not ordinarily been conceived of in any sufficiently complicated sense as capable of contributing to a man's success.

Gibbon appears before us first of all as the trustee of his intelligence. The book is "the history of my own mind" (p. 83), and he believes that in reviewing his "moral and literary character" he should "expatiate . . . on my private studies, since they have produced the public writings which . . . entitle me to the esteem and friendship of my readers" (p. 113). That is to say, the most obvious of those types of experience to which Roy Pascal refers is intellectual; and Gibbon traces his education with great care.

Gibbon could not remember a time when he could not read, write, and cipher (p. 55). In his very early years, however, his formal schooling was sporadic, for he was forever ill; "the care of my mind," he says, "was too frequently neglected for that of my health" (p. 55). Early in 1746, at the age of eight, Gibbon entered a school at Kingston-upon-Thames. "A school is a cavern of fear and sorrow," says Gibbon in a passage Lord Sheffield omits. There boys labor, "like the soldiers of Persia, under the scourge, and their education is nearly finished before they can apprehend the sense or utility of the hard lessons they are forced to repeat" (p. 69). At this school, at any rate, Gibbon learned little but Latin syntax, purchased "at the expense of many tears and some blood" (p. 58), before he was called home by his mother's death in 1747. Now for a time he came under the care of an aunt, Miss Catherine Porten. She became, he tells us, "the true mother of my mind," a fact that no doubt accounts for the strong affection he always felt for her. To her he owed his "invincible love of reading" (p. 61). Gibbon's maternal grandfather, James Porten, had recently absconded to escape his debts, and, in the months before his house and its contents were sold, Gibbon and his aunt ranged freely through the old man's library. There he "turned over many English pages of poetry and romance, of history and travels" (p. 62). That year, 1748, when he was eleven, was delightful—"the most propitious to the growth of my intellectual stature" (p. 62).

At last, however, the house was sold, and Miss Porten's rich relations, who "were not *absolutely* without bowels" (p. 62), set her up as a boardinghouse-keeper at Westminster School. There Gibbon followed her, as a boarder and a pupil. His attendance at classes was intermittent, for he was still sick, suffering now from a mysterious "nervous affection which alternately contracted my legs and produced, without any visible symptoms, the most excruciating pain" (p. 64). Various courses of treatment proved ineffective, until at last he spontaneously and permanently recovered. Now his father suddenly was "urged to embrace a singular and desperate measure" (p. 65), and in 1752 Gibbon, who had never risen beyond the third form at Westminster, was enrolled as a gentleman-commoner at Magdalen College, Oxford.

Gibbon's description of his state of knowledge at this juncture is well known. "I arrived at Oxford," he says, "with a stock of erudition that might have puzzled a doctor and a degree of ignorance of which a schoolboy would have been ashamed" (p. 68). Memorable as that sentence is, it is merely a summary. Gibbon details that "stock of erudition," and as he does so he makes clear the basis for the statement later in the book that "I *know* by experience that from my early youth I aspired to the character of an historian" (p. 137). During his time at Westminster, he had cherished his illnesses, for they gave him the opportunity to read as he wished; and "reading—free desultory reading"—was his greatest pleasure (p. 66). His interest "subsided by degrees in the historical line," a circumstance he attributes to his having been fascinated by successive volumes, issued serially, of the *Universal History*. From that work he proceeded to English translations of

Herodotus, Xenophon, Tacitus, and Procopius and thence "to the modern world: many crude lumps . . . passed through me like so many novels, and I swallowed with the same voracious appetite the descriptions of India and China, of Mexico and Peru" (p. 66). Such reading, so "vague and multifarious" (p. 67), did him little direct good. Indeed, as the vigor of his appetitive imagery suggests, his passion for these books, in its undisciplined strength, was perhaps an aspect of the illness it eased. But it had the effect of fixing Gibbon's mind before the age of sixteen on his great object. Even his "first introduction to the historic scenes which have since engaged so many years of my life" occurred during this time. On a visit to Wiltshire with his father in 1751, he happened on the *Continuation of Eachard's Roman History*, and it so fascinated him, he recalls, that "I was immersed in the passage of the Goths over the Danube when the summons of the dinner bell reluctantly dragged me from my intellectual feast" (p. 67).

The figure that emerges in his account of those years is, as Gibbon seems to recognize, somehow grotesque; it is a child historian, a boy whose father's visitors used to discover him "surrounded with a heap of folios of whose titles they were ignorant, and on whose contents he could pertinently discourse" (p. 67). Gibbon's detractors to the contrary, there is little smugness in this portrait of himself. It was ridiculous of him to presume "to weigh the systems of Scaliger and Petavius, of Marsham and Newton" in his "childish balance"; but there is pathos, too, in his statement that in those years "the dynasties of Assyria and Egypt were my top and cricket ball" (p. 68).

Gibbon's childhood, however painful it was, nevertheless issued happily in solid achievement, and he does not regret it. Eventually it did not even matter much that his fourteen months at Oxford turned out to be the "most idle and unprofitable" of his life (p. 72). The most serious consequence of those months was that, out of simple curiosity as much as anything else, Gibbon became a Roman Catholic. His father was outraged. Twenty-two days after his reception into the Church, Gibbon reached Lausanne, where from 1753 until 1758 he lived in the home of his tutor, M. Pavilliard, a Protestant clergyman. This was a most important period in his intellectual history, "the foundation of all my future improvements" (p. 98). By March of 1755, he had completed the first of the two educations that, he says, "every man who rises above the common level has received"; that is, he was through with teachers. Now he proceeded to the "second, more personal and important" of his educations, the one he got "from himself" (p. 98). Gibbon will not, "like the fanatics of the last age, define the moment of grace, but he cannot forget the era of his life in which his mind has expanded to its proper form and dimensions" (p. 98). In April of 1755 began the eight-month period "of the most extraordinary diligence and rapid progress" he ever experienced (p. 98).

In 1758, at the age of twenty-one, Gibbon was summoned home by his father. By this time, French, in which he "spontaneously thought," was more familiar to him than English (p. 95); in short, he "had ceased to be an Englishman," and his "opinions, habits, and sentiments were cast in a foreign mold" (p. 110). But that condition was to be corrected, at least in part. The great point was that now he was able to look ahead to a career in some fashion intellectual. His self-confidence was already so well established that he had begun to correspond, sometimes in Latin, with eminent European professors who answered him as an equal and of whom one welcomed and praised his emendation of a passage in Livy (pp. 104–105). It would take Gibbon some time and a number of false starts to find out just what his work would be; but the outlines of his future were beginning to define themselves.

His studies, of course, continued, but increasingly they were professional studies. The mind of the historian had been formed, though the history itself was yet to be conceived, and what Gibbon read now he read less for its own sake or even for the sake of its contribution to his intellectual culture than for its usefulness to him as a scholar. Now other men's books were things from which he did or did not get something to advance his own projects and ambitions.

> After glancing my eye over the design and order of a new book, I suspended the perusal till I had finished the task of self-examination, till I had revolved, in a solitary walk, all that I knew or believed or had thought on the subject. . . . I was then qualified to discern how much the author added to my original stock, and if I was sometimes satisfied by the agreement, I was sometimes armed by the opposition of our ideas (p. 122).

Rational skepticism of authority of the sort that this passage implies, is, as every scholar knows, necessary to a man who hopes to deal intelligently and productively with facts and ideas. And Gibbon had, even this early, another scholarly virtue—an accurate sense of his intellectual defects. It was not just knowledge that he had to acquire, but an appropriate literary style. His own, he knew, had been "corrupted by the long use of a foreign idiom," and to correct it he read "our English writers since the Revolution," particularly Addison and Swift (p. 122). He read the modern British historians, too. William Robertson's *History of Scotland* had just been published, and it "inflamed" Gibbon with the hope that he might write as well. Hume's history of England under the Stuarts was new, too, but its effect was sometimes to daunt him. Struck by Hume's "careless, inimitable beauties," he often closed a volume "with a mixed sensation of delight and despair" to return again, presumably, to his stylistic studies (p. 123).

But intellectual influences were not the only ones at work on him. From May, 1760, until December, 1762, he served as an officer in the Hampshire Militia. He regretted the "loss of so many busy and idle hours" and believed that his temper had been "soured by the society of our rustic officers" (p. 133). But this "wandering life of military servitude" did not prove a dead loss (p. 132). It made him, he says, an Englishman again. Moreover, the "discipline and evolutions of a modern battalion gave me a clearer notion of the phalanx and the legions, and the captain of the Hampshire grenadiers . . . has not been useless to the historian of the Roman empire" (p. 134). And there is something more here, something that redeems the pomposity of Gibbon's references to himself. It is hinted at in a sentence that occurs between his summaries of the evils and benefits of his months in the militia. "In every state there exists . . . a balance of good and evil," he writes. We must not be misled by the banality of this fragment of philosophy. Gibbon is expressing what he holds to be a general truth that explains the part that circumstance, accident, and even luck played in his life.

It is a theme to which he often returns. "I have drawn a high prize in the lottery of life," he says, and he means it.

> The far greater part of the globe is overspread with barbarism or slavery; in the civilized world the most numerous class is condemned to ignorance and poverty; and the double fortune of my birth in a free and enlightened country, in an honorable and wealthy family, is the lucky chance of a unit against millions (p. 204).

Even his grandfather's financial difficulties and his father's extravagance, subjects on which he sometimes comments harshly, turn out in the end to have been blessings, however thoroughly disguised. Enough was left him to ensure his independence; and yet he was not rich enough to be tempted to dissipation. This was for him a happy situation. "Few works of merit and importance have been executed either in a garret or a palace," he remarks in a passage Lord Sheffield suppressed; "in circumstances more indigent or more wealthy I should never have accomplished the task, or acquired the fame, of an historian" (p. 171). For similar reasons, he is glad that he did not take his stepmother's advice and study law. He was not suited to it, he believes, and therefore, had he followed her suggestion, he would "have been diverted from the labours of literature without acquiring the fame or fortune of a successful pleader" (p. 116). Gibbon is always aware of what, probably disastrously, might have been.

In Gibbon's view, in short, it was chance as much as talent and industry that formed the historian and hence the history. Nowhere is this clearer than in a phrase he uses to describe his first sojourn in Lausanne, that period when his mind "expanded to its proper form and dimensions." He speaks of it as a "fortunate shipwreck" (p. 110), and these two words, modifying one another almost in the manner of an oxymoron, define the moral tone of Gibbon's autobiography. At the end of his life, Gibbon can see his passage toward fame as having been, in a sense at least, a journey in the dark. There is humility in this, humility of a kind that, giving credit where it is due, allows him to claim for his will and intelligence the great share in his achievement they deserve.

But, though apparent misfortunes often turned out to be real blessings, the ambiguities of experience did not always favor him. By the time he came to compose his autobiography, his life had taught him a dark, Johnsonian lesson.

> The warm desires, the long expectations of youth, are founded on the ignorance of themselves and of the world. They are gradually damped by time and experience, by disappointment and possession (p. 207).

Style, says Gibbon on the first page of his book, "is the image of character," and few works exemplify this familiar notion more fully than this one, in which antithesis and balance reflect Gibbon's mature conviction that time and the event modify or even contradict the fears and hopes of the past, transforming weaknesses into strengths and ambitions into disappointments. Thus he characteristically reflected that, to balance the "first emotions of joy" that he felt on completing his history, there was the idea that he had taken "everlasting leave of an old and agreeable companion" and, further, that, however long his history should live, "the life of the historian must be short and precarious" (p. 195).

At the end of his life, he had achieved the fame he had sought. It brought solid satisfactions—"a name, a rank, a character in the world, to which I should not otherwise have been entitled" (p. 206). But, though he was happy, his was an "autumnal felicity" (p. 207). And, with the death of his old friend Deyverdun, though Gibbon was "in Paradise," he felt the pain of being there alone (p. 202). Possession, he says, is not much better than disappointment.*

The pathos of Gibbon's life is clear enough, the more so for his air of detachment about it, the sense his book communicates that his discovery that life is a melancholy enterprise was one he might have made without living it. As delicately as may be, he

* In *The Literary Art of Edward Gibbon* (Oxford, 1960), p. 149, Harold L. Bond remarks that "the balance and antithesis, the frequent use of comparison and contrast, which mark so much of Gibbon's writing, suggest emulation in the looser medium of prose of some of the artistic techniques found so frequently in the iambic pentameter couplets of the Augustan age." He is speaking of the *Decline and Fall*, but the observation applies with almost equal force to Gibbon's autobiography, especially to such paragraphs of it as the one discussed above. Gibbon's conception of himself is akin to his conception of the subject of his history, which in Bond's words (p. 61) is the "continued tension between the ideal and the real," a tension of which the other dominant figures of eighteenth-century culture were also plainly aware and to which they gave moving expression. In this connection, one thinks immediately of the opening lines of the second epistle of Pope's *Essay on Man* and of Johnson in "The Vanity of Human Wishes" and the first paragraph of *Rasselas*.

commends to us the notion that what experience and a lifetime of scholarship have revealed to him is the human sufficiency of those things that he had had almost from the start—such "solid comforts of life" as "a convenient, well-furnished house, a domestic table, half a dozen chosen servants, my own carriage, and all those decent luxuries whose value is the more sensibly felt the longer they are enjoyed" (pp. 171–172).

It has seemed to some of Gibbon's readers that the pleasure Gibbon takes in these comforts convicts him of bourgeois smugness; but the truth of the matter is something quite different. These are the highest blessings that even such a lucky man as Gibbon may reasonably expect, but they are not all he might desire. They are not what he had aspired to, but what he settled for. Gibbon acquiesces reluctantly in the judgment of experience on the great demands that youth makes of life and accepts, with a full sense of their value, the compensations that come his way. This is, in Gibbon's view, the path of wisdom, of however gloomy a sort. To the sympathetic reader, it must seem that to follow that path required considerable intellectual and moral courage, as does any other course of action that rejects what one holds to be the comforts of illusion.

This rigorous loyalty to what he believed to be reality accounts for the sometimes unpleasant severity of Gibbon's judgments of people and ideas. Like most of us, Gibbon almost instinctively conceives of reality as something harsher and less pleasing than appearance. It would be wrong to say that he is guilty (however differently from Mill and Wordsworth) of that fallacy of misplaced concreteness according to which only objects really exist (and they meaninglessly), the qualities we perceive in them being only the productions of our own minds. But surely that is the tendency of Gibbon's ideas. For Gibbon, it is particularly the emotions, especially those that bind us to other persons, that are deficient in point of reality. They can be felt, to be sure, and hence must be acknowledged in some sense to exist; but they are neither desirable for their own sakes nor useful in achieving rational—and therefore human—ends. Like the friction produced in a machine, the intensity of emotion is a function of the inefficiency of reason; one strives to reduce it, but recognizes that it cannot be eliminated. "My nerves are not tremblingly alive," says Gibbon, and he rejoices in the fact (p. 206). When he tells us that, in giving up Mlle Curchod, "I sighed as a lover; I obeyed as a son," we sense that he did not sigh very deeply nor obey very reluctantly (p. 109).

Such detachment permits him to say of the death of his father, for whom he felt real affection,

> The tears of a son are seldom lasting. I submitted to the order of nature, and my grief was soothed by the conscious satisfaction that I had discharged all the duties of filial piety. Few, perhaps, are the children who, after the expiration of some months or years, would sincerely rejoice in the resurrection of their parents, and it is a melancholy truth that my father's death, not unhappy for himself, was the only event that could save me from a hopeless life of obscurity and indigence (pp. 168–169).

Lord Sheffield omitted the first and last of these sentences in the interest of Gibbon's public character. They are uncomfortably reasonable remarks, and they typify Gibbon's consistent refusal to permit emotional convention to obscure the facts. What he says here is not cynical; it is merely true. The willingness to say it is a mark in Gibbon's favor, not one against him, for the moral self-awareness that prevents one from taking refuge in the comforts of grief and from afterward pretending (even to oneself) to that respectable emotion is not often a pleasant possession.

In Gibbon's childhood are many suggestions of why he so mistrusted emotions stronger than the sentiment of friendship. As we have seen, he was a lonely boy. He will "not pretend to lament" the five brothers who died in infancy (p. 49). Expecting him to die, Gibbon's parents had given each of them his name, and, though Gibbon does not say so, it seems likely that this tactic, diminishing his importance and almost dismissing him, would not have endeared a brother to him had one lived. There was almost no one in whom to invest his affections. At the death of his mother, he says, "some natural tears were soon wiped" (p. 59). Despite the Miltonic allusion, her loss was no expulsion from Eden: "As I had seldom enjoyed the smiles of maternal tenderness, she was rather the object of my respect than of my love" (p. 59). Aside from his aunt Catherine Porten, the only member of his family whom he can be said to have loved was his sister, whose early death he still regretted at the time of writing. But even here it is not so much the sister herself as a particular person that he misses (she is unnamed and described only as "an amiable infant") as it is the relationship that might have grown up between them. With a sister, he says, a brother may have

> a familiar and tender friendship with a female much about our own age, an affection perhaps softened by the secret influence of sex, but pure from any mixture of sensual desire, the sole species of platonic love that can be indulged with truth, and without danger (p. 49).

The negative aspect of this ideal is striking. The absence of danger is what he most praises. To love one's sister is to love prudently; it is like putting money into bank stocks or government bonds. For bolder ventures, Gibbon had no desire; and, for such timid ones as this, no real opportunity.*

* Some have speculated (though not, so far as I can determine, in print) that Gibbon may have been a homosexual and that his natural reluctance to disclose this fact accounts for the tone that he takes in discussing emotional commitment. Such a view his long intimacy with Deyverdun perhaps supports, though why a friendship between bachelors should necessarily be suspect is not entirely clear. All that is certain is that, for whatever reasons, he

Whatever the origins of his mistrust of emotion, this trait of character contributed to his ability to tell a certain kind of truth. His austerity of tone—in speaking of himself as well as others—helps persuade us that his assessment of the part persons and events played in the development of the historian is accurate. As we have seen, Gibbon is eager to acknowledge that he owed his success partly to luck, and that fact is a clue to the largest meaning of the book. The particular truth Gibbon's autobiography tells best is to be found in what he says about fortune.

I mean fortune in the sense, first of all, of "a fortune"—money. Few books deal more openly with the importance of money than Gibbon's autobiography. Its early pages concern themselves at length with how his family made and (during his grandfather's time) began to lose its money. The Gibbons were businessmen, and, for all his consciousness of rank and insistence on being known as a gentleman, Edward Gibbon saw nothing wrong in this. "Our most respectable families," he says, "have not disdained the countinghouse, or even the shop," for "gentility is not degraded by the exercise of trade" (p. 32). Gibbon's sense of solidarity with his ancestors comes in large part from a feeling that they—or their energies, at least—live on in their money. This sense of the life of a fortune, of money as something not separate from its possessor but as an aspect of his person and character, like health or force of mind, is strange to us, but to Gibbon it seemed perfectly natural. There is scarcely a distinction in his mind between his genetic and his financial inheritance. Hence, perhaps, the severity of his criticism of his father's

---

never entertained an abiding passion for a woman his own age. The chief feminine presences in his life were his aunt and his stepmother. The second of these women came on the scene just at the moment when he had separated from Susan Curchod. It may be that her "warm and exquisite sensibility" (p. 116) helped him forget the younger woman. Perhaps, as a friend of mine once suggested in conversation, Gibbon was grateful to his father for having done his marrying for him.

imprudence. Even the "decay and dissolution" of the elder Gibbon in his "last fatal summer" is described as a crisis in his affairs as much as in his health (p. 167). The dissipation of a fortune was to the son not mere foolishness, but vice, like dissipation in the sense of the waste of moral and physical powers.

In short, Gibbon recognizes that his lifework, the *Decline and Fall*, is, in an important sense, the result of his ancestors' industry. He acknowledges that he would never have written it if he had had to do so in hours stolen from a trade or a profession. He was happy, too, in not having too much; but the point is that his fortune was as intimately essential a part of his equipment as a historian as were his genius and his education. In him, the energies of generations of his family at last express themselves in the life of culture. Gibbon's autobiography is intensely interesting if for no other reason than that it speaks out about the alchemy that creates civilization, the process through which labor, money, and goods issue in art and ideas.

It is here that the notion of fortune as money involves itself with the notion of it as luck or chance. We examined earlier the part that fortune in the latter meaning of the term played in his life. It remains only to say how appropriate such a conception is as the informing principle of the autobiography of an historian—a man interested in the *fortunes* of things, in *how they turn out*. It is a principle in harmony with the historian's professional assumption that the true nature of events can only be understood in retrospect. Then reality sheds its disguise, and every item of experience, however happy or disastrous it may once have seemed, presents its consequences as its credentials. As the Greek poets insist, this conception of the operation of the world makes large allowance for the possibility of tragedy—a larger allowance than does the Christian notion, of which Gibbon was suspicious, that divine providence somehow makes all things work together for good, at least for those who love God. Gibbon's life was, to be sure, not tragic, but he knew that it might very well have been. In this knowledge he appears before us as a wiser and more modest person than we have sometimes supposed him.

For Gibbon, pain is not itself valuable; it does not give him access to an otherwise-unavailable reality. His fortunes and misfortunes mean only themselves. For him, the unavoidable accidents of life have resulted in a muted, provisional happiness, as the occasions of achievement. But they are accidents still—mere circumstance. Different as they are in other respects, in this view Gibbon and Roger North are at one. Both men are willing, though not eager, to accept what the world offers, and such willingness expresses the normal vision of life. North and Gibbon lack the taste for transcendence that the religious autobiographers to be examined next all share, the talent for extreme experience that brings the apocalypse home to the individual soul.

III

RELIGIOUS LIVES

The Example of Bunyan

"I preached what I felt," says John Bunyan of his sermons, "what I smartingly did feel." * He wrote what he felt as well; *Grace Abounding to the Chief of Sinners*, his autobiography, is the record and judgment of his sufferings. It first appeared in 1666, twelve years before *The Pilgrim's Progress*, and, if the more famous work had never been written, this book alone would have secured Bunyan a place in our literary consciousness. Indeed, *Grace Abounding* makes the highest kind of claims on our respect; for great autobiography, like tragedy, has more to teach us about experience than not to repeat it.

Grace Abounding is the very type of a remarkable genre—the vivid, vigorous autobiography of a Dissenter's soul. In it are all the virtues and almost none of the defects of what became, especially in humble, unliterary circles, a tremendously popular form. By 1725, the Quakers alone had published more than eighty confessions and journals. In the eighteenth century, Wesley, for the Methodists, urged the "Itinerant Preachers who were employed under his sanction to give him in writing an account of their personal history, including a record of their conversion to

* *Grace Abounding and the Pilgrim's Progress*, ed. John Brown (Cambridge, 1907), p. 84. Hereafter, citations of this work will appear in the text, in parentheses.

God."[1] Many complied, and a number of the narratives were published. Inevitably these attempts at autobiography resembled one another, reproducing with varying degrees of success the matter and manner of the masters and (for all practical purposes) originators of the form. Bunyan was one of those imitated, and for good reason: his work was early and pure.

Literarily, then, *Grace Abounding* was an exemplary work. In some sense it still is, despite the fact that, by the nineteenth century, the autobiographical impulse had become largely secularized, examination of the soul giving way to examination of the self. Indeed, it is the remarkable convertibility of those two terms, "soul" and "self," that allows us in the present age to feel the force of *Grace Abounding* and to see it as exemplary in another, to me rather more interesting, way.

For all its darkness, *Grace Abounding* is an inspirational work. That adjective is not nowadays a term of praise. And yet it fits Bunyan in a way we can accept. Surely his will to health of mind and spirit is something to emulate, and his relative success in achieving it is encouragement to hope that our power over ourselves is greater than we sometimes suppose. Bunyan testifies, to be sure, that that power is difficult to exercise. (Indeed, one great merit of the book is the severity of Bunyan's insistence that salvation, of whatever sort, is not easily come by.) Not only the life recorded in *Grace Abounding* but the very act of composing the book was in some sense of the phrase a noble work. "I have become to myself a soil laborious and of heavy sweat," says Augustine of his researches into memory.[2] To confront one's past and make sense of it is seldom pleasant, especially when one's life has been, as Bunyan's had, profoundly distressing in many of its passages. And yet the enterprise may be privately rewarding. The personal value for Bunyan of his transactions with his past was that they rendered it intelligible and therefore bearable.* "*I*

* In *John Bunyan, Mechanick Preacher* (New York, 1934), pp. 34–35,

can remember my Fears, and Doubts, and sad Months with Comfort," he says in a passage that sums up the terrors and benefits of self-examination; "*they are as the head of Goliath in my hand*" (p. 5). There is a promise in this, and that promise and the disciplined will and moral intelligence that Bunyan displays everywhere in *Grace Abounding* are what make it so large and worthy a book.

Bunyan's book is remarkable for, among other things, what it does *not* tell us. His first wife is unnamed, and her importance to him seems to have been chiefly that she brought to the marriage two religious books that interested him. He scarcely mentions his children except to say that parting from them was painful, "the pulling the Flesh from my Bones" (p. 97). Bunyan became a Baptist, but he says almost nothing of the theological doctrines that set that sect apart from other branches of Dissent. Indeed, he does not mention even his own baptism, though we know it occurred.* But these omissions are, as it turns out, not a vice but a virtue. Bunyan's silences constitute a formal principle. Everything is excluded but what touches on his inner life. The trials he underwent and their meaning—and nothing else—are the matter of his book.

Bunyan was a battlefield. For him, of course, the dangers of the conflict that raged there were spiritual: Satan and he "did so tug and strive; he pulled and I pulled; but, God be praised, I got the better of him, I got some sweetness from it" (p. 67). Modern readers, however, are likely to be more comfortable with the

---

William York Tindall is eager to suggest that a leading purpose of Bunyan was to advertise his own salvation, thus providing for himself the credentials of a prophet. Perhaps so. But Tindall's seems an unnecessarily ungenerous view. See F. R. Leavis' largely unfriendly notice of Tindall's attitude toward Bunyan in *The Common Pursuit* (London, 1962), pp. 204–207.

* The Bedford congregation of which Bunyan became a member offered but did not insist on baptism of new members. Roger Sharrock, *John Bunyan* (London, 1954), p. 30.

roughly equivalent notion that the book is an account of a man's struggle with his neurotic constitution. Indeed, it is in this notion that our interest in him is grounded. Bunyan shares in the illness that, under the tutelage of Freud, we have come to accept as the condition of man. To say this is not to explain away him and his book. Though what he shares with us is the beginning of our interest in him, it is *only* the beginning. His uniqueness is what claims our serious attention, and that uniqueness is the moral force of which his artistic power is an expression. Of any writer we may say, with Lionel Trilling, "that whatever elements of neurosis he has in common with his fellow mortals, the one part of him that is healthy, by any conceivable definition of health, is that which gives him the power to conceive, to plan, to work, and to bring his work to a conclusion." [3] So extreme are the mental sufferings set down in *Grace Abounding* that the very existence of the book testifies to Bunyan's power over pain; that is, to his essential health.

As early as the age of nine or ten, Bunyan was afflicted with dreams of devils and even wished himself a devil, that he might be a tormentor rather than a victim (pp. 8–9). The first great crisis he records, however, and the one that casual readers seem to remember most clearly, occurred after his marriage. One Sunday, he heard a sermon on Sabbath-breaking, and "at that time I felt what guilt was, though never before, that I can remember." By afternoon, he had shaken off his depression. But he could not escape it long, for

> the same day, as I was in the midst of a game at Cat, and having struck it one blow from the Hole, just as I was about to strike it the second time, a Voice did suddenly dart from Heaven into my Soul which said, *Wilt thou leave thy sins and go to Heaven, or have thy sins and go to Hell?* At this I was put to an exceeding Maze. Wherefore, leaving my Cat upon the ground, I looked up to Heaven, and was as if I had, with the Eyes of my understanding,

> seen the Lord Jesus looking down upon me, as being very hotly displeased with me, as if he did severely threaten me with some grievous Punishment for these and other my ungodly Practices (p. 12).

Bunyan immediately concluded that he was beyond redemption.

> I was persuaded, I could never attain to other Comfort than what I should get in sin. . . . Wherefore I found within me a great desire to take my fill of sin, still studying what sin was yet to be committed, that I might taste the sweetness of it (p. 13).

Here is the beginning—or at least the first open statement—of the compulsive attraction Bunyan always felt toward evil. Throughout *Grace Abounding* he need no more than hear of a sin to wish, against all the restraints of his conscience, to commit it. Even when he became a preacher he had to fight hard against the impulse to blaspheme in the pulpit (p. 88). At the time of writing, however, Bunyan was perfectly aware of how irrational his feelings had been that Sunday afternoon. Satan, he says, "stilly and slily supplieth [some men] with such despair, that though not much guilt attendeth Souls, yet they continually have a secret conclusion within them, that there is no hopes for them" (p. 13). Unwarranted despair, or fear and guilt without an object, is spiritually dangerous. Their result, as Bunyan acutely remarks, is a "benumbing of conscience," the *accidia*, or spiritual torpor and sloth, of which moral theology speaks (p. 13).

This generalized anxiety arising from his disproportionate sense of guilt perhaps helps to explain the odd circumstance of Bunyan's being weaned away from that innocent village amusement, bell-ringing. This occurred a year or so after his first experience of sin. His conscience "beginning to be tender," he began to think bell-ringing vain and therefore quit it. Now, as at other times, the action he has come to think a sin fascinates him even more strongly than when he considered it a simple delight. He "hankered" after it. That antique verb, implying as it often seems to an unreasonable longing after something unsuitable and improper, precisely communicates the new quality in his desire to ring those bells. "Wherefore I should go to the Steeple house, and look on it, though I durst not ring. But I thought this did not become *Religion* neither, yet I forced myself, and would look on still" (p. 15). Here, translated into moral terms, is something very like the response of the acrophobe who compulsively, yet charged with terror, approaches the edge of a high rooftop and looks down. His fear, as any such person will testify, is mixed with desire—a tortured hankering. There is the wish to fall and the wish to refrain—terms that clearly have a moral as well as a physical significance. Freud touches on these twin significances when describing the anxety dreams of women; [4] and it is even possible to find in Luke's account of the temptations of Christ a suggestion that moral acrophobia of the sort Bunyan felt is what Satan vainly hoped to discover in Jesus as they stood on the pinnacle of the temple. One of Christ's perfections is his exemption from neurosis. He is the first sane man since prelapsarian Adam.

Gradually now, Bunyan cut himself off from his old pleasures—not only bell-ringing, but swearing and dancing. He had become, he says, a "brisk Talker" in matters of religion. But one day in Bedford he came upon "three or four poor Women sitting at a door in the Sun, and talking about the things of God"; their joyous conversation convinced him that they had found a "new world" from which he was excluded (p. 16). His mind was now so fixed on divine things that "it lay like a *Horse-leech* at the *Vein*," yet still he could not convince himself that he had real faith and was one of the elect (p. 17). Satan presented to his mind the notion that "those good people of Bedford . . . were all that God would save in those parts" (p. 24). As always, Bunyan here is ingenious in finding reasons to torment himself, but his pain is nonetheless real for that. His spiritual loneliness was extreme.

At about this time, Bunyan made the acquaintance of John Gifford, the minister of the Bedford congregation of moderate Baptists, and in 1633 he joined that church. The worst of his storms were, however, still ahead of him. The most agonizing of these was the temptation to "sell Christ." For about a year, Bunyan says, "I could neither eat my food, stoop for a pin, chop a stick, or cast mine eye to look on this or that, but still the temptation would come, *Sell Christ, . . . sell him, sell him*" (p. 42). At last, one morning as he lay in bed, "I felt this thought pass through my heart, *Let him go, if he will;* and I thought also, that I felt my heart freely consent thereto." Now he fell down "as a Bird that is shot from the top of a tree, into great guilt, and fearful despair" (pp. 43–44).

For two years, he was convinced of his certain damnation. He details the moment of his deliverance (however temporary) from that certainty. At about "ten or eleven o'clock one day," as he was "walking under a hedge," a particular sentence "bolted in on me, *The blood of Christ remits all guilt.*" At this, "the Tempter did lear and steal away," and for a short time—two or three hours only—Bunyan was encouraged (p. 44). This episode typifies the events in his life for some time thereafter. He constantly alternated between hope and despair, each turning being announced by his lighting on some isolated line of the Bible that seemed to promise now redemption and now damnation. "Comfort now, and Trouble presently," as he puts it (p. 64). At length, however, after much searching of the Scriptures, he was able to convince himself that hope was possible, permanently and reasonably so. "And now remained only the hinder part of the Tempest" (p. 71).

Bunyan makes it clear that he misunderstood his sufferings at the time he was undergoing them. He thought then that, in "selling" Christ, he had committed the unforgivable sin of Judas. Even his senses suggested this conclusion, for in his terror he felt such a "clogging and heat" in his stomach that at times it seemed his "breast bone would have split asunder"; this made him think of Judas, "*who, by his falling headlong, burst asunder and all his bowels gushed out*" (p. 50). But really (as Bunyan knew by the time he came to write) his despair was not a rational response to the fact of his sin; rather, his despair was itself his sin. Selling Christ was bad enough, to be sure; but the "foolish practice, of putting by the Word of Promise when it came into my mind" was, he tells us in a summary passage, the root of his difficulties (p. 76). The divine economy of God's wrath, he now understands, made the sin of "proneness to desperation" its own punishment (p. 53).

There is a literary and a moral point here. One mark of the superiority of *Grace Abounding* over many other spiritual or otherwise introspective autobiographies is its analytic tone. For good autobiography is not merely a chronicle of experience, but a judgment of it. How things seemed to Bunyan at the moment they happened he makes very clear; but against the appearance of things he sets the reality that retrospection has shown him. The judgment that Bunyan passes on his despair is the key to a proper understanding of his book. Bunyan now recognizes that from the first his sense of guilt had been out of all proportion to what he had deemed his offense. As he said in his remarks on that Sabbath game of tip-cat, hopelessness is something that Satan "stilly and slily supplieth." Bunyan's appetite for evil, we infer, expressed his wish to find some object for his guilt to fix on, some crime to supply the other half of the moral equation. He had confused real guilt with something that feels just like it—free-floating neurotic anxiety. Now he holds that to give in to unwarranted despair, to accede to sickness, is itself a sin. In Bunyan's somber view, irrational remorse calls for real repentance. The first serious obstacle to the pilgrim's progress is the Slough of Despond; his duty is to struggle out of it.

It is right, then, to speak of Bunyan's experiences and his account of them as expressing his desire for wholeness and health of mind. Considered thus, the benefits that Bunyan gained from his struggle are intelligible. "I never saw those heights and depths in Grace, and Love, and Mercy, as I saw after this temptation," he says. "When *Job* had passed through his Captivity, *he had twice as much as he had before*" (p. 77). Bunyan here testifies to the truth of William James's observation that the

> securest way to the rapturous sort of happiness of which the twice-born make report has as an historic matter of fact been through a . . . radical pessimism. . . . [The sufferer,] when saved, is saved by what seems to him a second birth, a deeper kind of conscious being than he could enjoy before.[5]

That deeper consciousness finds utterance in *Grace Abounding* in the moral profundity of Bunyan's judgment of himself and the heroic rigor of his notion that what we might excuse as illness is a sin.

Bunyan does not make these great claims for himself. It has been remarked that to call oneself the Chief of Sinners is prideful; but if Bunyan's title lays him open to such a charge, nothing else in the book does. He is relentless about his early errors, and he is not complacent about his spiritual state at the time of writing. Everywhere but in that title he is unaffectedly modest. The heroism with which he endured his sufferings and, even more, with which he judged them is very great; but it appears indirectly, as an aspect of the manner of his narrative.

Our praise of Bunyan's style, when we are speaking of its serious virtues and not simply its pleasant quaintness, turns quickly into praise of his character. Despite Bunyan's silence about the external details of his life, the prose of *Grace Abound-*

ing is rich with physical fact. The significant events of Bunyan's progress take place against a background, however hastily sketched, in which the reader discerns the plainness of Bunyan's circumstances. They occur as he sits "upon a Settle in the Street," "as I was walking to and fro in a good man's shop," or "as I was standing at a Neighbours Shop-window . . . playing the Madman, after my wonted manner" (pp. 58, 52, 43). Bunyan's spiritual voyage is through a world barren of comforts, but full of the stubbornly uninspirational things of rural life. "*Have you never an Hill Mizar to remember?*" Bunyan asks his readers in the Preface (p. 5). That they have not is no excuse. "*Have you forgot the Close, the Milk-house, the Stable, the Barn, and the like, where God did visit your souls?*" So with himself. One day,

> as I was betwixt *Elstow* and *Bedford*, the temptation was hot upon me, to try if I had Faith, by doing of some Miracle: which Miracle, at that time, was this; I must say to the *Puddles* that were in the Horse-pads, *Be dry;* and to the *dry places, Be you the Puddles:* And truly, one time I was going to say so indeed; but just as I was about to speak, this thought came into my mind; *But go under yonder Hedge and pray first, that God would make you able:* But when I had concluded to pray, this came hot upon me; That if I prayed, and came again and tried to do it, and yet did nothing notwithstanding, then to be sure I had no Faith, but was a Castaway, and lost. Nay, thought I, if it be so, I will never try yet, but will stay a little longer (p. 20).

Bunyan does not think it odd that something as prosaic as a muddy lane should be the scene of a spiritual test nor that the great miracle he is tempted to perform is no more than the drying up of a puddle.

It is possible to take pleasure here in condescending to the poor tinker who, with apparent naïveté, avoids the pain of proving the weakness of his faith by refusing to put it to a trial. But such pleasure is illegitimate. The real force of the passage lies in the disparity between the quality of Bunyan's experience and the humble circumstances in which it takes place—a disparity that is most moving. Further, there is the point that, if even an innocent hoofprint may be the occasion of sin, this is a dark world indeed. The fact that Bunyan does not think to mention either the pathos or the threat implicit in this passage—that to him they are not, in any sense of the word, remarkable—testifies not to his naïveté, but to a stoic kind of courage. For him, those two implications of the event go without saying.

But, when he wishes to do so, Bunyan is ingenious at finding in the world of objects and actions equivalents for his subjective states.* Thus he used to "flounce towards" the promises of salvation "as the Horses do towards sound Ground, that yet stick in the Mire" (p. 76). This is not merely picturesque. Bunyan's lively figures are in the service of the narrative of his sufferings; the more closely his language allows us to approach what his life felt like to him, the more fully we recognize the heroism of the man who could withstand such experiences. We must not miss the force of the fact that Bunyan is able to endow almost every motion of his mind with physical presence. His spiritual troubles seem to have presented themselves to him in just such concrete terms. So it is that Satan seems to pull at his clothes and speaks to him in the rough voice of a countryman: "*You are very hot for mercy*," Satan says tauntingly, "*but I will cool you. . . . Many have been as hot as you for a spurt*" (p. 35). Even the scriptural texts that so puzzled him have life and palpable force of their own. Their comforts come in "hints, touches, and short visits." He receives "a sweet glance from that in the fifth of second

* The names of towns and persons in *The Pilgrim's Progress* seem less like allegorical inventions when one recalls that on a map of England there is a Newbold Revel and that in Bunyan's time a man called Praise-God Barban but christened Unless-Jesus-Christ-Had-Died-For-Thee-Thou-Hadst-Been-Damned was a prosperous contractor in London. See Roger North's *Autobiography* (London, 1887), p. 52.

Corinthians." Certain sentences are "bigger than others be." Once conflicting texts "bolted both upon me at a time, and did work and struggle strangely in me for a while" (pp. 37, 36, 64, 66).

It becomes clear that this "work and struggle" in him is no mere manner of speaking. All his energies come into play. In the most vivid passage of this sort, Bunyan tells us that, in combating Satan's insistence that he "sell" Christ, he had "for whole hours together . . . been forced to stand as continually leaning and forcing my spirit against" the temptation; "by the very force of my mind," he continues, "in labouring to gainsay and resist this wickedness, my very body also would be put into action, or motion, by way of pushing with my hands, or elbows" (p. 43). Throughout *Grace Abounding*, the whole man is involved in what is, in the first instance, a spiritual struggle.

Bunyan could have "*stepped into a Stile much higher than this*," he says in the Preface; "*but I dare not: God did not play in tempting of me; neither did I play, when I sunk as into a bottomless pit . . . : wherefore I may not play in relating of them, but be plain and simple, and lay down the thing as it was*" (p. 6). To be plain and simple and lay down the thing as it was—in short, to tell the truth—is a large endeavor. I have suggested that Bunyan's manner of expression makes the felt quality of his experience so clear to us that we recognize his powers of endurance to be heroic. The resolute truthfulness of his book testifies to still another aspect of his heroism. I mean the courage of mind with which Bunyan on the one hand resists false comfort and intellectual temptation and on the other compels his experience to render the meaning he is sure lies hidden in it.

We saw this kind of courage expressed in the severe judgment Bunyan passed on his despair, and to that we shall return in a moment. But Bunyan was capable of such intellectual rigor even during his periods of deep distress. It was tempting, for instance, to think that Christianity, like Mohammedanism, was "*but a Think-so*" and that there would be no Day of Judgment (p. 32); as Satan put it to him, "*For if these things should indeed be true, yet to believe otherwise, would yield you ease for the present*" (p. 49). Bunyan persisted in denying himself that ease, though (considering the misery that belief was causing him) the temptation must have been great. He had found that, unless his guilt were removed "the right way, that is, by the Blood of Christ," he grew "rather worse for the loss of . . . trouble of Mind, than better" (p. 29).

He had to reduce even his dreams to moral intelligibility. He tells us of one in which he found himself alone and cold at the foot of a walled mountain on whose sunny slopes sat some of the blessed people of Bedford he so envied. After some searching, he discovered "a narrow gap, like a little doorway in the Wall," and at last, "by a sidling striving" and headfirst, he managed to pass through it (pp. 20–21). A Freudian interpretation, which this dream clearly invites, might suggest a number of things about Bunyan's private desires and their connection with his religious longings.* But such revelations are in a sense beside the point. For Bunyan, the mountain is the church, the wall is the Word,

* See *The Interpretation of Dreams*, trans. James Strachey (New York, 1955). The "plans, maps and so on," Freud says, that some psychoanalytic patients draw to illustrate their dreams often seem (in a fashion that will not surprise students of metaphysical poetry) to represent the human body. Freud's experience leads him to generalize that "many landscapes in dreams, especially . . . wooded hills, may clearly be recognized as descriptions of the genitals" (p. 356). And, more particularly, among the examples in *The Interpretation of Dreams,* Freud records one in which the male organ is symbolized by a person and the female by a mountain (p. 366). Bunyan's struggle to gain entrance through the "little doorway" is suggestive, especially in his insistence that it was accomplished "by a sidling striving" and headfirst. But it is not necessarily suggestive of a desire for the ordinary sexual act. It is warmth and comfort that Bunyan is struggling toward, not "satisfaction." Dreams that concern "passing through narrow spaces," Freud suggests, are often "based on phantasies of intra-uterine life, of existence in the womb and of the act of birth" (p. 399).

and the gap in the wall is Christ (p. 21). It does not matter that Bunyan's interpretation of his dream is too abstract to be satisfactory. The great point is that he did interpret it. Bunyan conceives it almost a sin to let any fact of his experience remain unexplained to himself.

Such passages, though they are very pointed, would mean little were not the whole energy of the book directed so fiercely against the false comforts of self-indulgence. But that is its direction. One must not rest in error, Bunyan says, but pursue understanding. To neglect to do so is impious, for it implies the acceptance of meaninglessness as a possibility, a notion incompatible with the fact that the data of experience are somehow God's dealings with us. To attempt to find the meaning but to fail is, in Bunyan's view, just as bad. Hence his severity toward his early sufferings. They were an incorrect response to reality, imputing a wrong meaning to it. Bunyan reminds us of the austere, invigorating truth that we are responsible for what we think and feel. A moral act is an act of mind, and an act of mind is a moral act.

I have been speaking of two kinds of courage: Bunyan's power to endure suffering and his will to make that suffering intelligible to himself—to withstand and to understand. They are not separable in him, of course. In both the psychological and moral senses of the term, he is a man of great integrity. It is this, I think, for which we chiefly admire him; to return to the word I used early in this chapter, it is what makes him exemplary.

I intend that word "exemplary" quite strictly as meaning fit to serve as a model. This has not, in any very intelligent acceptance of the notion, been the part that Bunyan has been called on to play. His patience under suffering has been admired, of course, and we have been urged to imitate it. But with that admiration has often gone a certain condescension. "Poor patient Bunyan," William James calls him, and his highest praise is that eventually Bunyan's life "was turned to active use." [6] We nowadays commonly resist or underrate or simply fail to perceive the heroic, as James does here: it makes us uncomfortable in its implicit reproach. Thus, we prefer to associate ourselves with Bunyan's weakness, with his neurotic misery which is so recognizably like ours, not with that strength of mind by which he achieved the wise sanity of which many of us in our own lives have despaired. In so doing, we are in fact being untrue to the deepest meaning of those very notions, whose purest expression is the Freudian psychology, by which we justify this submission to weakness. For only apparently have we license to submit. Psychoanalysis is, to be sure, in its descriptive aspect deeply wounding to our pride. It and other cultural forces have denied us forever Bunyan's faith in the almost perfect intelligibility of experience. But in intention psychoanalysis is first of all therapeutic; that is, it is hopeful. It has a program in the service of health; it is active and prescribes activity; and the activity it prescribes is precisely the exercise of mind to narrow the dominion of the irrational.

This meaning of psychoanalytic thought is familiar enough, theoretically. But apparently we need to be reminded of it all the time. It sometimes seems that, whenever we come to apply Freudian ideas to moral matters, we prefer to dwell on that aspect of them that, drawing attention to our very great limitations, seems to excuse passivity and acquiescence rather than that that encourages us to action. Thus perhaps part of the enthusiastic welcome Norman O. Brown's remarkable book *Life against Death*[7] received in some circles was due, not to its great particular merits, but to the fact that it seemed to issue from a horror at culture and a sense that health is impossible in society that contemporary readers are too predisposed to accept. Brown's book is not that simple, but the response to it often is.

The encouragement Freud offers is real encouragement; that is, it is heartening. To ignore it is a large mistake, for to do so is to cherish an insufficient sense of human possibility. Bunyan, as we have seen, thought that a sin, and there is the greatness of his book; he was right in any terms we choose. Theologians have always condemned the hopelessness that attends an excessive sense of guilt. Freud would concur in this judgment. If there is any moral meaning at all in his ideas, it flows first from the notion that relative health of mind is a possibility, however difficult of attainment, that, indeed, it is life. Bunyan's exemplary life, like the good life described and lived by Freud, is a life of suffering, struggle, and judgment. It is at last an intellectual life, in a broad sense of that term, an intellectually heroic life, and in it power and virtue are one. Toward that unity even Freudian man—perhaps *especially* Freudian man—may proceed. Now, as in Bunyan's time, it is our duty to be saved.

George Fox and Other Quakers

Besides Bunyan's, there survives outside the consciousness of antiquarians and bibliographers one other autobiographical work by a seventeenth-century hero of religion—George Fox. If literary importance is judged by the number of imitators a work has, his *Journal* outshines even *Grace Abounding*. But in this instance the quality of the influence is very much at issue. Fox's work was easy to imitate, but difficult to imitate well. The difficulty, it seems likely, was owing to the diffuseness of the *Journal* and its consequent tendency to resolve itself into its elements under the eye of the imitator, who in his effort to emulate his master identified one aspect of the book with the whole.

The *Journal* does not have the effect on the reader of a unified work of art. What comes down to us is a compilation of various manuscripts, chief among them being the *Spence MS.*, dictated by Fox to his stepson-in-law in 1674 or 1675, and *The Short Journal*, dating from 1664. The edition known to Fox's followers was edited by Thomas Ellwood (himself an autobiographer, as we shall see) and appeared in 1694.* Though this was the edi-

* John L. Nickalls, ed., *The Journal of George Fox* (Cambridge, 1952)

tion that influenced Fox's imitators, the differences between it and the best modern versions are not so great as to make it necessary to use the earlier text here. It was not details that Fox's followers adopted, but the main outlines, the major emphases. And, in any event, influence is, for the moment at least, a secondary consideration. What we need to know is just what sort of book the *Journal* itself is.

The titles of these imitations are, to be sure, an aid to such knowledge, for these titles advertise the categories of their contents and the contents of their source. One, published in 1750, is called *A Brief Narrative of the Life, Convincement, Conversion, and Labours in the Gospel-Ministry of . . . John Bancroft*. Another, published in 1710, is entitled *An Account of the Convincement, Exercises, Services and Travels of Richard Davies*. Even closer to Fox is the account of the life of Margaret Fell, his wife, which deals with her "birth, education, life, conversion, travels, services, and deep sufferings." In all these, the emphasis falls on certain early interior religious experiences that culminate in conversion and thereafter on the work in the world and the suffering of these Quakers as they spread their doctrine. Usually, the first and more interesting section is by far the shorter. And so, in every respect, with George Fox.

In his *Journal*, Fox does three things—the first two of them very well. He records his spiritual experiences; he describes, with considerable drama and occasional flashes of humor, his encounters with repressive authority; and he recounts his travels in detail. As a reporter of experience, he is a fit rival to Bunyan. Like Bunyan, Fox was born in humble circumstances, the son of a weaver who, though he never came to share his son's religious views, was known to his neighbors as "righteous Christer" (p. 1). From his earliest years, Fox was of a sober temperament, with "a

pp. vii–x. Hereafter, citation of this work will appear in parentheses in the text.

gravity and stayedness of mind not usual in children" (p. 1). He summarily dismisses these years in three pages and begins his serious account with his departure from home in September of 1643, when he was just twenty. He traveled now through neighboring counties, seeking men who shared his still unclearly defined religious notions. It was a time of trial and temptation continuing for several years. He enjoyed "openings" from God—a term he and his followers used for personal revelations—and "was sometimes brought into such an heavenly joy that I thought I had been in Abraham's bosom" (p. 10). But, as late as 1647, there was more darkness in his life than light. He tells us:

> I fasted much, and walked abroad in solitary places many days, and often took my Bible and went and sat in hollow trees and lonesome places till night came on; and frequently in the night walked mournfully about by myself, for I was a man of sorrows in the times of the first workings of the Lord in me (pp. 9–10).

Like Bunyan before him and later Cowper and others, he was tempted to the belief that he had committed the unforgivable sin against the Holy Ghost (p. 14). Certain Biblical texts were great puzzles to him; but now and again God inspired in him an understanding of them. Once, in Nottingham, he suddenly knew "that the natures of those things which were hurtful were within, in the hearts and minds of wicked men" (p. 19). In a moment, he had acquired a sense of the inwardness of evil, an intuitive knowledge of how it felt to be a sinner, though he remained sinless himself. Even a saint must somehow have the experience of sin. "It was needful I should have a sense of all conditions, how else should I speak to all conditions; and in this I saw the infinite love of God" (p. 19).

Intuited experience of this sort had for Fox the sound practical value he had anticipated, as one example will demonstrate. One morning,

> as I was sitting by the fire, a great cloud came over me, and a temptation beset me; but I sat still. And it was said, "All things come by nature"; and the elements and stars came over me so that I was in a manner quite clouded with it. But inasmuch as I sat still and silent, the people of the house perceived nothing. And as I sat still under it and let it alone, a living hope arose in me, and a true voice, which said, "There is a living God who made all things." And immediately the cloud and temptation vanished away, and life rose over it all, and my heart was glad, and I praised the living God (p. 25).

He had been tempted to believe that material causes are sufficient to explain the universe, and he had overcome that temptation. When, soon afterward, he met and converted a group of people who were victims of that belief, he "saw that it was good that I had gone through that exercise" (p. 25).

At about this point, an event occurred that seems to have been transcendently important to Fox's religious convictions and to his confidence in his calling. A man named Brown "had great prophecies and sights upon his death-bed of me," Fox writes, and, at the man's burial, Fox fell into a faint or trance so nearly resembling death that for fourteen days afterward people flocked to see him. "For I was very much altered in countenance and person as if my body had been new moulded or changed" (p. 20). In short, Fox died and was resurrected. In his trance, he descended into Hell and rose to Heaven:

> And I saw into that which was without end, and things which cannot be uttered, and of the greatness and infiniteness of the love of God, which cannot be expressed by words. For I had been brought through the very ocean of darkness and death, and through the power and over the power of Satan, by the eternal glorious power of Christ. Even through that darkness was I brought, which covered-over all the world, and which chained down all, and shut up all in the death. And the same eternal power

> of God, which brought me through these things, was that which afterwards shook the nations, priests, professors, and people (p. 21).

Here, in the fullest imaginable sense of the term, is a Christian experience; no wonder it convinced Fox of his vocation and others that he was "a young man that had a discerning spirit" (p. 21).

Fox's commission from God was an immediate communication.

> I did not see by the help of man nor by the letter, though they are written in the letter, but I saw them in the light of the Lord Jesus Christ, and by his immediate Spirit and power, as did the holy men of God, by whom the Holy Scriptures were written (p. 34).

Fox is making the highest claims for the dignity and authority of private experience. Even the Scriptures are of less moment than the inner light vouchsafed by God, of which he has unquestioning and unquestionable knowledge.

> Yet I had no slight esteem of the Holy Scriptures, but they were very precious to me, for I was in that spirit by which they were given forth, and what the Lord opened in me I afterwards found was agreeable to them (p. 34).

He very nearly says that the authors of Scripture are in the right because their inspiration is conformable to his, not, as a less confident man might have put it, that his notions are right because they are conformable to the Bible. God had permitted him to see "the depths of Satan on the one hand" and "on the other hand, the divine mysteries of his own everlasting kingdom" (p. 34). From this time onward, Fox trusted absolutely the motions of his own heart.

More often than not, Fox decided even the humblest practical questions by listening to his inner dictates. Matters of doctrine were, of course, always thus delivered, including the famous command that Quakers " 'thee' and 'thou' all men and women, without respect to rich or poor" and the prohibition of "hat-honour" which was to cause him and his adherents much trouble (p. 36). More and more, however, the divine communications concerned the "convincement" and regulation of others and less and less the ordering of Fox's own spiritual constitution. Now and again, God might have both objects in view. On such occasions, commands had the intensity of a vision.

A famous instance of this sort of divine communication occurred one day in 1651 when, "walking in a close with several Friends," Fox "espied three steeplehouse spires." A "steeplehouse"—he will not call it a church, reserving that word for more mystical uses—was always abhorrent to him; it always, as now, "struck at my life." The nearby city, his companions told him, was Lichfield; and now "the word of the Lord came to me that I might go." Escaping his friends' notice, Fox "went over hedge and ditch" toward the city, stopping only to pull off his shoes (though it was winter) because "the word of the Lord was like a fire in me." As he reached the town,

> the word of the Lord came unto me again to cry, "Woe unto the bloody city of Lichfield!"; so I went up and down the streets crying, "Woe unto the bloody city of Lichfield!" Being market day I went into the market place and went up and down in several places of it and made stands, crying, "Woe unto the bloody city of Lichfield!", and no one touched me nor laid hands on me. As I went down the town there ran like a channel of blood down the streets, and the market place was like a pool of blood (p. 71).

Even Fox felt this errand to be an odd one; when he had finished, he could only wonder "why I should go and cry against that city," for as far as he knew it was no bloodier than any other. Later he learned that he had been responding to a "sense" of the blood "of a thousand martyrs in Lichfield in the Emperor Diocletian's time" (p. 72). The point is that Fox was unwilling to let his strange experience pass unexamined. Like Bunyan, though not in the same degree, Fox insists on the final rationality of divine manifestations.

And, open as Fox was to communications from God, he could be skeptical of them, especially when an enemy claimed to have received one. His skepticism sometimes has a remarkable shrewdness about it. Once, for example, when a Ranter, to flatter him, claimed to have had a vision of him sitting in a great chair before which the Ranter bowed down, Fox "told him it was his own figure: and said unto him, 'Repent, thou beast' " (p. 81). The sharpness of this retort is perhaps not good therapeutic practice, but the insight it expresses seems psychoanalytically sound.

Perhaps the most intense of the visions that came to Fox in the course of his mission occurred in 1671. Dreaming that he walked with Friends in an open field, he suddenly knew that beneath his feet "was a mighty vault top-full of people kept under the earth, rocks, and stones." He directed his companions to dig up the field and release the imprisoned people. As a parable of his conception of his ministry, Fox's dream is clear thus far. But it continues rather more mysteriously.

> And I went on again and bid them dig again, and Friends said unto me, "George, thou finds out all things," and so there they digged, and I went down, and went along the vault; and there sat a woman in white looking at time how it passed away. And there followed me a woman down in the vault, in which vault was the treasure; and so she laid her hand on the treasure on the left hand and then time whisked on apace; but I clapped my hand upon her and said, "Touch not the treasure." And then time passed not so swift (p. 578).

Here is Fox's complacence at the admiration of his followers, a theme to which he recurs frequently in the *Journal*. But here, too, is the beauty of phrase—"a woman in white looking at time how it passed away"—that characterizes the *Journal* at its best. Fox understands this vision, he says; he insists on understanding his mysteries. But he will not—perhaps because he cannot—explain it. "They that can read these things must have the earthy, stony nature off them. . . . I leave them to the right eye and reader to see and read" (p. 578). But what is to be seen and read he has rendered at once wonderfully clear and absolutely incommunicable.

Shortly after his "resurrection," Fox had received the command from God "to go abroad into the world, which was like a briery, thorny wilderness, and when I came in the Lord's mighty power . . . the world swelled and made a noise like the great raging waves of the sea" (p. 33). The second of the three things Fox does in his *Journal* is to give a lively and detailed account of the noise and raging that he encountered as he went about the world. As is well known, the persecution of the early Quakers was vigorous; the harassment, nearly unceasing. Fox's account of one trial he stood and the imprisonment that followed will exemplify his skill at dramatizing a scene and describing a place, a skill no less marked than that he displays in describing his inner experiences.

The trial took place at Launceston in 1656; the judge was Sir John Glynne, Lord Chief Justice of England under Cromwell; and the cause arose from the Quakers' refusal to take an oath, even to the truth. This refusal to swear caused the Quakers great trouble. Even sympathetic judges were often frustrated in their desire to free them by their unwillingness to swear to their intention, unquestioned by these magistrates, to behave peaceably. But in this case the judge was unfriendly, and what enraged him most was the disrespect it seemed to him that the Quakers were showing by refusing to doff their hats. His mistake was, as Fox's account makes clear, in allowing himself to be drawn into a discussion.

"Why do you not put off your hats?" said the judge.
And we said nothing.
"Put off your hats," said the judge again.
But we said nothing.
Then again the judge:
"The court commands you to put off your hats."
And then I replied and said, "Where did ever any magistrate, king, or judge from Moses to Daniel command any to put off their hats when they came before them into the courts . . . ? Or show me where it is written or printed in any law of England where any such thing is commanded; show it me and I will put off my hat."
And then the judge grew very angry and said, "I do not carry my law books on my back."
Then said I, "Tell me where it is printed in a statute book that I may read it."
Then said the judge, "Take him away, prevaricator, I'll firk [trounce] him" (p. 243).

After a recess presumably occupied in research, the judge recalled the prisoners. "'Come,' said he, 'where had they hats from Moses to Daniel? Come, answer me, I have you fast now,' said he." At this point Fox's shrewdness declares itself. Perhaps no hats are mentioned in the early books of the Bible, but in the book with which Fox's challenge had ended they are.

Then I said, "Thou mayest read in the third of Daniel that the three children were cast into the fiery furnace by Nebuchadnezzar with their cloaks, hose, and hats on. And you may see that Nebuchadnezzar was not offended at their hats."
He cried again, "Take them away, gaoler" (p. 244).

Though Fox gained his debater's point, as usual he lost the case. Having overturned a number of his enemies' accusations, he and his companions were at last fined for refusing to doff their hats and imprisoned until the fine should be paid.

Now comedy makes way for more somber matter; they were confined in the depths of the prison, in a chamber ominously named "Doomsdale,"

> a nasty stinking place where they said few people came out alive; where they used to put witches and murderers before their execution; where the prisoners' excrements had not been carried out for scores of years, as it was said. It was all like mire, and at some places at the top of the shoes in water and piss, and never a house of office in the place, nor chimney (p. 252).

The jailer would not provide them clean straw nor permit them to clean the place. When they burned a little straw at night to drive away the smell, smoke rose to a room above occupied by ordinary prisoners and thence to the quarters of the jailer himself. This put him in such a rage

> that he stamped with his foot and stick and took the pots of excrements of the prisoners and poured it down a hole a-top of our heads in Doomsdale, so that we were so bespattered with the excrements that we could not touch ourselves or one another, that our stink increased upon us. He quenched our straw with it. And he called us hatchet-faced dogs and such names as we never heard in our lives. What with the stink and what with the smoke, we were like to be choked and smothered, for we had the stink under our feet before but now we had it on our backs. In this manner we stood all night for we could not sit down in the place being so full of the prisoners' excrements (p. 253).

The strong effect of this account—one of several such in the *Journal*—is the result of Fox's literary tact, his willingness to let things and men speak for themselves. His style answers perfectly to what is required of it, the rendering of a hard physical reality consisting of things immediately available to the senses without the interpretive or clarifying assistance of rhetorical figure. In the description of "Doomsdale," I find no metaphor and only one simile (and that a perfunctory one—the place is "like mire"). Here are smoke, straw, urine, excrement, chamber pots, noise, a candle, and the dark. The name of the place is, to be sure, a metaphor. Life in "Doomsdale" is an undecorated sermon on Hell.

Plain-spokenness is the virtue of Fox's style. This is true even of those introspective and visionary passages examined earlier, figurative though they are. They are full of similes and metaphors, often ones copied from or inspired by the Bible. But these are very active figures. He speaks of "openings," of the steeple as having "struck at" him. One feels that such terms are not used in a mere manner of speaking, but quite literally, to refer to psychic events so vivid as to be scarcely distinguishable from physical ones. When Fox "sees" a truth, the reader infers that it was in every sense a visionary experience, even when no vision is described. The visions that he does fully describe are solid and particular, however mysterious their significance. That "woman in white" who sat "looking at time how it passed away" is looking at something that she can see, something that is *there*. When his companion touches the "treasure on the left hand," Fox notices that "then time whisked on apace." The crucial word here is "whisked"; its homeliness, its plain actuality which implies an equal actuality in its subject, endows that intangibility, "time," with a physical existence, for anything that can whisk away can be here.

One other aspect of Fox's style does not, however, always have such fortunate effects. That is his often-monotonous linkage of sentences with the conjunction "and." Passages organized in this way can be very powerful. The piling-up of parallel clauses can have extraordinary hortatory force; it can hypnotize. It gives the impression of something chanted, a strophe. Fox's vision of the "woman in white" is ordered in this fashion, and that fact partly accounts for the strength of the passage. But more often, instead of hypnotizing or otherwise controlling the reader's mind, repetitiveness of this sort simply lulls. It is partly this that renders Fox's account of his travels—the third of his projects in the *Journal*—so boring.

> And from Bristol I passed through the counties to Olveston and Nailsworth, and Nathaniel Cripp's where there was a large meeting and several soldiers came, but were quiet.
>
> And so from thence we passed to Gloucester through Friends, visiting their meetings. And after we had our meeting in Gloucester which was peaceable, though the town was very rude and divided, for one part of the soldiers were for the King and another for the Parliament. And as I passed out of the town over the bridge, Edward Pyott was with me, the soldiers there said they were for the King: and after we were passed away and the soldiers understood it was me, they were in a great rage, and said had they known it had been me they would have shot me with hail shot rather than I should have escaped them; but the Lord prevented their hellish design. And so I came to Colonel Grimes's house where we had a large General Meeting, and the Lord's truth and power was set over all, and people were established upon the rock and settled under the Lord Jesus Christ's teaching (p. 369).

The *Journal* contains hundreds of pages of this sort of narrative. This is history of a primitive sort. It brings to mind the *Anglo-Saxon Chronicle*, for here as there the writer is the prisoner of time and apparently almost incapable of articulating any relationship between ideas and events more complicated than mere sequence. This is the defect of that virtue of Fox's style, simplicity; here is language in a primitive state—vigorous, clear, direct—but insufficiently supple, syntactically unsophisticated.

The sources of this difficulty are not difficult to find. Opening the Bible almost at random, one comes upon chapters—chapters of narrative, especially—in which verse after verse proceeds in this way. More important still, the *Journal*, we recall, was not written but dictated. One peculiarity of this mode of composition is surely that the author's attention is fixed more closely on the fact or event that he holds in his imagination or memory at any particular instant than on its relationship to other facts or events. For him, what has gone before has subsided into silence, vanishing from precise recollection more fully than it can for the author who sets down his sentences one by one on paper. The "and" that begins so many of Fox's sentences signifies not only the sequence of events he is narrating but the sequence of mental events as he composes. Memory is a democratic process; in it, great and small are equated because each receives equal attention in the moment of recollection. Each is totally and exclusively, though temporarily, in possession of the consciousness.

Fox's is an oral style, with the virtues and weaknesses of informal discourse. He composes sentences, not paragraphs. This fact is a clue to the inferiority of Fox's *Journal*, magnificent though it is in detail, to Bunyan's *Grace Abounding* and to some of the works that we have yet to examine. The weakness of the *Journal* is a weakness of form, of proportion. The reader gets no help from the shape of Fox's book; it has none. Certain moments, certain scenes are more memorable than others; but Fox does not order his record so as to make decisive passages in his life declare their decisiveness unmistakably to the reader. For instance, that "death" and "resurrection" on which we dwelt earlier was surely the supreme crisis in Fox's spiritual life. It confirmed his intuitions about his calling; it established his confidence in God's special favor to him. Yet his account of it occupies only one paragraph (though a long one), and nothing in the text calls direct attention to the transcendent importance of the experience. The reader must con Fox's book very carefully to determine what matters most in it. Fox could remember his past in all its rich actuality; but he could not—at least he did not—give his record a form that could extract from that past its full meaning. His failing is a failing of judgment—of literary judgment in the first place, for he did not make the book what it could have been, but of moral judgment also, for, in exercising literary judgment on his past, the autobiographer is coming to an understanding of it, an enterprise that has its dangers as well as its rewards. For the autobiographer, the exercise of literary judgment is a moral act. Fox shirks the task, and for that reason his *Journal* is inferior to Bunyan's as an instrument of moral knowledge, for himself and for us.

As might be expected, where Fox fails, his followers, less gifted than he, fail also, and more completely; and, where he succeeds, they often do not. The feature of Fox's *Journal* most frequently imitated is the weakest, most tedious element of his work —the account of travels in the ministry. In a typical work, James Dickinson writes:

> We took Shipping for *Whitehaven* on the 26th of the twelfth Month 1692, and the Lord wonderfully favored us with his living Presence, which caused Tears of Joy to flow. We landed safe at the *Highlands* in *Scotland* on the 15th of the second Month 1693, and from thence travelled into *Cumberland* home, where we staid but a few Weeks until we took our Journey to the Yearly Meeting at *London*. . . .[8]

All is barren chronicle and automatic jargon, and there is page after page of it.

Even such a work as Dickinson's includes a sketch of his early life and spiritual experiences; but it is perfunctory (six pages out of 170) and uninteresting. Like Fox's, his wanderings are dictated immediately by God: "a Concern was upon me from the Lord to go. . . . I felt drawings in my mind." [9] He uses such phrases over and over again, but he never tells us how a "Concern," a "drawing," feels. He is too abstract to tell us what we really want to know. One thing is, however, clear despite his prose: the duties that he laid on himself may be described as psychic tensions pressing for discharge. Once Dickinson was moved to address and reprove a Presbyterian congregation. The prospect so frightened him that for several days he neither slept nor ate. Still the pressure increased: "and the Word of the Lord was as a Fire in my Bones, that I had no Peace till I had given up to it." [10] At last he did as God required and received the rough treatment that he had expected, which in itself gave him a certain satisfaction. "And finding myself clear, I said, *Your Blood be upon your own Heads, for I am clear of it:* So I came away in great Peace of Mind." [11]

The language is Fox's, and so is the structure of the experience: a sudden "drawing," a period of tension, a crisis, and a sense of being blessedly "clear." But there is no reason therefore to doubt that Dickinson in fact underwent his "exercises" (the Quaker term for such experiences) in just this way. What is remarkable is the similarity between such an "exercise" and an entirely self-seeking sexual experience. Some Quaker journals, recounting a series of monotonously similar and ferociously intense encounters of the sort that Dickinson's typifies, have the same power to fascinate and yet deaden the mind as the autobiography of a wandering amorist.

Nothing, of course, could have been further from the intentions of these pious journalists. The point is that many of these autobiographies are interesting only for what they accidentally reveal, not for what they set out to tell about their authors. Our interest in them is clinical, not literary. Still, they are evidence of the tendency of the autobiographical impulse to put a man in touch, however fleetingly or inconsequentially, with the dark corners of himself. And an occasional work of this inferior order contains here and there a passage that rises to the dignity of Fox at his best or Bunyan. An example is the *Journal* of John Woolman, an eighteenth-century American Quaker.

Woolman's book illustrates the defects at the same time as it exemplifies the strengths of the minor Quaker journal. Having "often felt a motion of love to leave some hints in writing of my experience of the goodness of God," Woolman writes at the outset, "now, in the thirty-sixth year of my age, I begin this work." * In the beginning, he is writing in 1755. The early pages are an orderly review of a large portion of his life, and as such they constitute an autobiography in the ordinary sense of the term. But, somewhere in Chapter Three (Page 38 at the latest), he catches up with time. Henceforth, for the seventeen years and nearly two hundred pages that remain, his book more nearly resembles a diary than it does an autobiography. This casual mixture of modes and the consequent disproportionate emphasis on the years of travel and ministry reduce, in my opinion, much of Woolman's *Journal* to stupefying dullness.

Like the other Quakers, Woolman depended entirely "upon the daily instructions of Christ, the Prince of Peace." [12] His steady and humble confidence that he does in fact receive such instructions and that there is nothing extraordinary in this—that it is within the power of *every* Christian to receive them—makes Woolman a more attractive saint than some. He feels "drawings" of the spirit until, like Fox and Dickinson, he discharges them. But in Woolman the sexual analogy is not so strong. In Dickinson's accounts, release, the effect on *himself* of doing his duty, seems nearly everything; the purpose of the psychic tension that gathers in him is simply its own discharge. Not so with Woolman. For him, peace usually follows only on the accomplishment of some real good—for example, persuading a man to free his slaves. Woolman's spiritual experiences are less self-regarding than Dickin-

* John Woolman, *The Journal and a Plea for the Poor*, intro. Frederick B. Tolles (New York, 1961), p. 1. Tolles reproduces in an illustration the original—and typical—title page: *A Journal of the Life, Gospel Labours and Christian Experiences of . . . John Woolman.*

son's and some of Fox's, less likely to end as the satisfaction of a psychic need than as the fulfillment of some self-imposed but rational obligation.

Woolman's "exercises" were no less intense for that. The account of one of his visions demonstrates the vividness of Woolman's interior life. Further, it exemplifies his insistence that his private experience should become available and valuable to others.

This vision occurred during one of his many missionary expeditions. One night, "being in good health, and abroad with Friends visiting families," he went to bed at "about the usual time with me"; he slept, but soon awoke to meditate for a time "on the goodness and mercy of the Lord, in a sense whereof my heart was contrited." Again he slept, and again he awoke. This time, though "it was yet dark, and no appearance of day or moonshine," just as he opened his eyes

> I saw a light in my chamber, at the apparent distance of five feet, about nine inches in diameter, of a clear, easy brightness, and near its centre the most radiant. As I lay still looking upon it without any surprise, words were spoken to my inward ear, which filled my whole inward man. They were not the effect of thought, nor any conclusion in relation to the appearance, but as the language of the Holy One spoken in my mind. The words were, CERTAIN EVIDENCE OF DIVINE TRUTH. They were again repeated exactly in the same manner, and then the light disappeared.[13]

The reader is struck by the meticulousness of this account. The quality of the light, its apparent size and distance from him —these details are noted with the exactitude of a scientist or at least of a man reporting to an audience whose skepticism he acknowledges to have its rights. Woolman's notation of the attendant circumstances is likewise in the service of the credibility of his account. He was in good health; he had gone to bed at the usual time; he had meditated on divine things but not so long as to have exhausted himself. He insists that the circumstances were normal, and yet this extraordinary thing occurred. How else are we to explain it except as a manifestation of God? The tone here differs from that of a Fox or a Dickinson. Woolman is not concerned to exhibit himself as one specially favored by God. His purpose is to give his experience an effect beyond himself. The standard objection to the doctrines of Quakers has always been that inner experience is unverifiable. Woolman attempts as far as he is able to meet that objection. It is a fact that the confidence of some in their intimate relationship with God bred in them a certain arrogance; a thing was true because they knew it to be true, and the audience might take it or leave it. In contrast to such people, Woolman displays an admirable humility in his decent respect for the opinions of mankind.

This humility is expressed in his accounts of other spiritual illuminations. At eighteen, his faith had been confirmed by a mystical perception of the unity of all things. "I looked upon the works of God," he says, "and an awfulness covered me. My heart was tender and often contrite, and universal love to my fellow-creatures increased in me." [14] Characteristically, Woolman was not content to rest in contemplation; knowledge of truth had to issue in ethical action. Religion properly begins in "an inward life," but it must express itself in the exercise of

> true justice and goodness, not only towards all men, but also towards the brute creatures; that, as the mind was moved by an inward principle to love God as an invisible, incomprehensible Being, so, by the same principle, it was moved to love him in all his manifestations in the visible world; that, as by his breath the flame of life was kindled in all animal sensible creatures, to say we love God as unseen, and at the same time exercise cruelty towards the least creature moving by his life, or by life derived from him, was a contradiction in itself.[15]

The corollary of the dignity with which he here perceives the creatures to be endowed is resignation of the claims of the ego to special importance. A vision vouchsafed him near the end of his life gives the clearest expression of that necessity. "In a time of sickness," Woolman

> was brought so near the gates of death that I forgot my name. Being then desirous to know who I was, I saw a mass of matter of a dull gloomy color between the south and the east, and was informed that this mass was human beings in as great misery as they could be, and live, and that I was mixed with them, and that henceforth I might not consider myself as a distinct or separate being. . . . I then heard a soft melodious voice, more pure and harmonious than any I had heard with my ears before; I believed it was the voice of an angel who spoke to the other angels; the words were, "John Woolman is dead." [16]

The words "John Woolman is dead," he discovered, "meant no more than the death of my own will." [17] He speaks as though that death had just taken place. *Henceforth* he must not consider himself "a distinct or a separate being." But he really never had considered himself one. This willingness to sink his self in the divine will had shaped his work in the world, which was to encourage men to express in their actions and institutions the spiritual egalitarianism that he believed to be the reality underlying all appearances. For Woolman, all creatures were innately precious. Slavery, for instance, because it reduces men to things, was a metaphysical as well as a moral evil. Opposition to it was his most consistent preoccupation throughout his life; and it was an opposition ultimately founded in mystical experience.

Woolman's is a flawed book, for the reasons suggested earlier. But in it those notions of the self of which the Quakers and Methodists and others made so much are expressed at their calm best. The primacy of private experience is unquestioned; only in the recesses of the self is the truth made known, for reality centers there. But in the experience of that reality the self becomes, paradoxically, selfless; the ego is burned away, abolished. Such experience is a beginning, not an end. It must commend itself to the world as a spiritual possibility. (Such commendation is one task of autobiography among the sects; the testimony of enough honorable people will at last convince skeptics of the reality of such experiences; a Dr. Johnson may not believe *one* Methodist, *one* Quaker, but ten?—twenty?—a hundred?) And it must validate itself in action. For all its imperfections, Woolman's *Journal* embodies these notions. It is a less remarkable book than Fox's, but only because it is less vigorous and various.

To be sure, occasional Quakers wrote autobiographies of a sort different from any of these. Thomas Ellwood, Fox's editor, was brought up a gentleman, and his autobiography conveys, no doubt accidentally, a sense of the social awkwardness that such a person felt on becoming a Quaker, the "Friend" and fellow prisoner of many persons born beneath him.[18] The *Memoirs* of David Ferris, an American, details the intellectual process by which he was converted from Presbyterian to Quaker beliefs.[19] But these are exceptions. Quaker autobiography, at its most typical, is exemplified by the works of Fox, Dickinson, and Woolman. And Quaker autobiography at its best is exemplified in the first and last of these.

Fox's and Woolman's books affirm the authority of inward illumination and thereby claim for the experiencing self a high dignity as the aspect of man directly in touch with truth incapable of other communication. The same applies to the Methodists and to at least one Evangelical, William Cowper. But the lesson Woolman quietly accepted—that what the self learns is the necessity of its own annihilation—these others struggled to resist. The extreme experiences to be examined in the next two chapters express the efforts of the self to assert its own integrity, at whatever cost, and the eventual frustration of those efforts, a frustration that at last will seem a victory.

Some Methodists' Lives

Methodist autobiography, though very like that of the Quakers, is not so coherent a body of work. One reason is that the Wesleys produced no great seminal model that could serve the faithful as Fox's *Journal* served the Quakers. John Wesley kept a journal. Volume after volume survives; but Wesley's is an even more unwieldy work than Boswell's, and therefore, however arbitrarily, I shall exclude it from consideration here. There is an even better reason for excluding other Methodist journals: their intention was entirely private. Such a work was written exclusively for the author's own edification (though occasionally one was published posthumously). Rigorous self-examination was part of the "method" of Methodism, and the keeping of diary-journals was simply a discipline that many of the faithful undertook to enforce a daily confrontation of themselves.

Thus, one Mary Gilbert, who died in 1768 at the age of seventeen and whose diary had gone through six editions by 1813, performed on paper "the needful duty of self-inspection" for the sake of discerning "the imperfection of her best performances." Mary, according to her anonymous editor, was "not afraid of being singularly pious,"[20] and this statement is no more than the truth. Each entry focuses to the exclusion of virtually all else on the state of her soul. "My soul was in a cold, dead frame, and so it continued all the day," she writes; or "My soul was much blessed"; or, of a sermon, "I was much tempted with drowsiness under the word, yet some parts of it were greatly blest to me." [21] The struggle is a day-by-day affair; no victory is permanent. Almost the only external event she records is her visit to a garden in a village named Grislington. "Some part of it represents a field of battle, a general's tent, with cannons all round it, a mount, a tower, a draw-bridge, and everything to resemble a camp of soldiers." But even this curiosity is an occasion for moral reflection: the Uncle Toby who owns it is a clergyman, and the garden is a sign to Mary that, reprehensibly, "he had very little else to think of." [22]

Her style is unimpressive. "I found a blessing while dressing," she writes at one point.[23] And one feels that she has fallen too much under the influence of pulpit rhetoric; she refers to the body of a dead girl as "her sweet agreeable tabernacle." [24] Still, though it is easy to make fun of her book, works of even this sort testify to the fact that in these years people were coming increasingly to live most intensely in the privacy of their feelings. But Mary Gilbert's diary has value *only* as evidence. It is merely history, of however private a sort, and in this it is unlike good autobiography.

Despite Wesley's example and the natural tendency of Methodist introspective discipline to find literary expression in diaries, a fair number of Methodists composed autobiographies. In a passage quoted earlier, the Methodist editor Thomas Jackson recalled Wesley's suggestion that his preachers write accounts of their lives.[25] Among those who did so was George Whitefield, who, if not a Wesley, was nevertheless an important early leader of the Methodist party.

Whitefield wrote his book aboard ship during his 1738 trip to America, when he was only twenty-four. Essentially it is an account of how he came to find himself embarked on his mission.

"I have simply told what I was by Nature, as well as what I am by Grace," he writes, thus grounding in theology a theory of biography of which a Roger North or a Johnson would approve and at the same time indicating, by the tenses of the parallel verbs, his sense of the structure of his life.[26] At the very beginning, Whitefield accuses himself of such sins as card-playing, novel-reading, and stubbornness. His childhood was a mixture of these vices and mysterious intimations of salvation and a calling; he always loved to play at being a clergyman. But it was not until he reached Oxford and came under the influence of the Wesleys that he became earnest about religion. Whereas before he had been "busied in studying the Dry Sciences, and Books that went no farther than the Surface," he now "read only such as entered into the Heart of Religion, and which led me directly into an experimental knowledge of *Jesus Christ.*" [27]

That word "experimental," much used among the Methodists and Evangelicals, is an interesting one, for it roots knowledge of divine things in experience—"heart experience," as it is sometimes put. But states of soul other than blessedness were also known "experimentally." Not long after he adopted the Wesleys' principles and began to live by their rule, Whitefield fell suddenly into deep depression. He felt, he says, an "Impression and Weight upon my Breast"; his soul, in terms that describe passages in the lives of all these autobiographers, was "barren and dry." Whitefield felt himself "a Man locked up in Iron Armour." [28]

In light of this phrase, it is no wonder that John Stuart Mill should have likened his depressed state of mind to a Methodist's, for these words of Whitefield's perfectly express that sense of insulation from the world and the inaccessibility of feeling of which Mill was complaining. And Whitefield's phrase also sums up that paralysis of the emotions from which Matthew Arnold believed it to be the special power of Wordsworth's poetry to free us. Whitefield could, however, find no way out of his suffering except to force it to a crisis. His pains, he says, were the result of carrying the life by rule to an extreme—a temptation that is one of Satan's strategies for corrupting good things.[29] The cure, strangely, was to press on still harder. In Lent, he fasted so rigorously that he collapsed. For seven weeks he was sick, but the sickness was the occasion of his recovery of spiritual health. One day, the victim of a stubborn thirst, he imitated the crucified Christ by crying out, "I thirst! I thirst!" And now "I found and felt in myself that I was delivered from the Burden that had so heavily oppressed me!" So happy was he that for some time he "could not help singing Psalms" wherever he was.[30]

Whitefield's is not the most interesting of the Methodist autobiographies. But it illustrates certain important notions. One of these is suggested by his youth at the time he composed it. The crisis in his faith once passed, the major events in his life were behind him. Nothing more could happen that would matter nearly so much, and hence, even at twenty-four, he was ready to write his life. Thus, tacitly as well as explicitly, he emphasizes the supreme importance of these experiences to a Methodist. And Whitefield is helpful in defining the nature of the crisis. For him, his despair was a matter of being out of touch with his feelings, and his deliverance was a restoration of emotional tone to life. "I found and felt in myself that I was delivered," he wrote in the passage just quoted. The doubling of the verbs is significant. Alone, "I found" might refer simply to an intellectual conviction. But the addition of "felt in myself" declares and locates the experiential aspect of the new knowledge—"experimental" in the sense that Methodists praised. Moreover, Whitefield's accidental discovery that, for him at least, to pass out of despair meant to persevere in the course of life that had brought on that depression illustrates a truth to which others in these pages bear witness, that one may have to explore one's hell to its most extreme reaches. The exploration is not desired, but it is sometimes necessary.

What such a hell could be is one of the things suggested in the autobiography of John Haime, "Late Soldier in the Queen's Regiment of Dragoons" and a Methodist preacher.[31] This brief work—it is only thirty-seven pages long—is to my mind the most charming of the Methodist lives. And it is remarkable for, among other things, the direct and conscious influence on it of Bunyan's book. Soon after joining the army in 1739, Haime came on a copy of *Grace Abounding*. "I read it with the utmost attention, and found his case nearly resembled my own. . . . I bought it, and thought it the best book I ever saw." [32]

It is clear from the earliest pages that indeed Bunyan's case did resemble Haime's. Like Bunyan, he came of a humble family. Haime's father was a gardener. His uncle was a button-maker, and Haime followed this trade for a time, but without satisfaction in it. Like Bunyan, he was at an early age given to "cursing, swearing, lying, and sabbath-breaking." [33] Haime's first intense spiritual experience was experience of evil. As he did Bunyan, Satan tempted Haime to blaspheme and convinced him that his case was hopeless. Now and then, "the great tremendous God" would interpose his grace for a time, but for some years, like the author he so admired, Haime underwent the torture of temptation and despair. Even in church, he was so tempted

> that it was as much as I could do, to avoid blaspheming aloud. Satan suggested, "Curse him, curse him!" perhaps a hundred times. Then he suggested, "Thou hast sinned against the Holy Ghost." But still I cried unto God, though the deep waters flowed over me, and despair closed me in on every side.[34]

Nor is this the only instance of an almost perfect parallel with Bunyan; Haime sometimes hesitated to enter a church "lest the Church or the tower should fall upon me." [35]

The accounts of both Haime and Bunyan derive part of their force from the humble circumstances in which incidents in their lives occurred, circumstances that the authors carefully, but unself-consciously detail. One day, Haime's employer, a tanner, sent him to fetch a load of bark. Returning, Haime

> was violently tempted to blaspheme, yea, and to hate God; at length, having a stick in my hand, I threw it towards heaven against God, with the utmost enmity. Immediately I saw in the clear element, a creature like a swan, but much larger, part black, part brown. It flew at me, and went just over my head. Then it went about forty yards, lighted on the ground, and stood staring at me. This was in a clear day, about twelve o'clock: I strove to pray, but could not. At length God opened my mouth.[36]

The strangeness of this manifestation is set off against the ordinariness of the setting, as in that passage in *Grace Abounding* where Bunyan considers attempting the miracle of drying up a mud puddle. The occurrence is described quietly, factually; the odd color of the bird and its distance from him are important details. The time of day, the quality of the light, the atmospheric conditions are all noted. Haime's purpose, like the Quaker Woolman's, is to make credible the marvelous. Spiritual modesty is at work here. His attention is not principally on John Haime, the specially chosen recipient of a divine warning, but on the manifestation itself, the thing that God did.

God's dealings with him are so exclusively Haime's subject that, like other religious autobiographers, he scarcely mentions his family. As he marched away with his regiment on Christmas of 1738, the thought of parting with his wife and children almost broke his heart, but we never hear of them again. For a time, now, he was still tormented by doubts of God's mercy to him. One intermission of his doubt is interesting, for it suggests how the religious autobiographies achieved their intended purpose. Haime writes that one day as he was reading

> in what manner God manifested himself to Mr. Gennick, I cried out, "Lord, if there be any mercy for *me*, reveal it to me!" I was

> answered by so strong an impression on my heart as left me without a doubt. . . . Immediately my soul melted within me, and I was filled with joy unspeakable.[37]

It was work of this sort that Haime no doubt hoped his own book might do.

He tried to do such work in person. John Wesley advised him in a letter: "Speak and spare not: declare what God has done for your soul." [38] This imperative is obviously designed to provoke laymen to preach, and what they are to preach is their experience. Wesley's words are another piece of evidence that the autobiographical impulse was close to the heart of early Methodism. It was at any rate close to John Haime's heart. "I did speak, and not spare, with little interruption," he writes[39]—and this in the midst of a war. Haime took part in the battle of Dettingen, an engagement in the War of the Austrian Succession, in which he was under fire for seven hours. In bivouac in the months that followed, Haime gathered about him a small company of like-minded men who, under his direction, began to proselytize the army. Haime himself was a great field preacher, often appearing before a thousand officers and men. "Was there ever so great a work before, in so abandoned an army?" he inquires.[40] The faith he inspired reached its highest pitch at the battle of Fontenoy, when, by his account, his followers charged eagerly toward the enemy shouting, "I am going to my Beloved." When Haime's horse fell beneath him, he "walked on, praising God. . . . I was as full of joy as I could contain." [41]

This exaltation did not last. For three years, Haime had known himself to be forgiven. But he again fell into sin. "My fall was both gradual and instantaneous," he acutely observes. Having grown negligent in "watching and prayer," he one Sunday violated his scruple against "buying or selling the least thing on the Lord's-Day." At this, a sense of wrongdoing quite literally struck him: "I was carried to a hospital, just dropping into hell." Now it seemed to him that the whole visible universe was his enemy.

> The roads, the hedges, the trees, everything seemed cursed of God. Nature appeared void of God, and in the possession of the devil. The fowls of the air and the beasts of the field, all appeared in league against me.[42]

This profound alienation, this sense of absolute isolation from the good, is not at all unusual among these autobiographers, nor is Haime's notion that repentance will not help, that he is unique in being beyond hope of salvation. Bunyan experienced it; so did Fox, though it was not so prominent in his account; and so did William Cowper, to whose account we shall come soon. But perhaps no one expresses it more directly than Haime does in these three sentences above. And certainly no one speaks more honestly of another part of the experience, the return that the sufferer makes against his affliction: "I was angry at God, angry at myself, and angry at the devil."[43] Sinfulness is denial, negation—and the experience of that condition Haime fully and clearly expresses.

His sufferings lasted seven years. As Bunyan, Fox, Wesley, and others had often done, Haime used to open his Bible at random in hope of chancing on some healing text; but he found none. He continued his efforts to convert others, though (like Bunyan again) he was often

> tempted to curse, and swear, and blaspheme, before and after, and even while I was preaching. Sometimes while I was in the midst of the congregation, I could scarcely refrain from laughing aloud, yea, from uttering all kind of ribaldry and filthy conversation.[44]

At length he was discharged from the army. At Haime's request, Wesley appointed him a traveling preacher, an occupation that he followed for some time, occasionally accompanying Wesley himself (who "knew how to bear with me") on his journeys.[45] Eventually Haime declined into what Wesley called "a worn-out Preacher" and retired to an informal chaplaincy in the employ of a Mr. Hoskins. There one morning his peace of soul was suddenly restored. "I was afraid I should alarm the whole house with the expressions of my joy," he writes; "I had a full witness from the Spirit of God, that I should not find that bondage any more. Nor have I ever found it to this day." [46]

Haime's account has many virtues. One of them is its brevity. The rest are Bunyan's. Even the clarity and simplicity of Haime's style, adequate to its occasions but in no way "literary," resembles his master's. The influence, we have seen, is direct and conscious. The question that arises is this: was Haime's life actually as similar to Bunyan's as his little book is to *Grace Abounding?* Is it not possible that the power of *Grace Abounding*—a power that Haime acknowledges—shaped Haime's recollections when he came to write? It is impossible to be certain, and it may not matter. If, on the one hand, the influence on Haime's memory was great, that fact demonstrates no more than that *Grace Abounding* was a pattern of spirituality for Haime. On the other hand, if Haime's experiences had in fact the Bunyanesque quality that his book suggests they had, we then have independent evidence of the currency of this variety of the inner life. In either case, the earlier work stands as a paradigm, a fact that makes it important not only to the student of literature but to the historian of culture. The Bunyanesque self was flourishing in mid-eighteenth-century England, experiencing what Bunyan had experienced and valuing it in the same way.

More important, at the moment, than such considerations is the evidence that Haime provides about the nature of the sin against the Holy Ghost of which so many of these writers held themselves guilty. His account declares it to be an act of negation, an unconsciously desired—unconsciously willed, if the phrase is possible—separation of the self from the good.* But negation and

* See the sermon of John Newton, the friend and spiritual adviser of William Cowper, quoted by Maurice J. Quinlan in "William Cowper and

separation in the interests of what? To that question the autobiographies of Silas Told and, even more plainly, William Cowper suggest an answer.

The autobiography of Silas Told is one of the most variously interesting of the Methodist accounts. It must be admitted that the interest is not altogether owing to his descriptions of the inner life. As a young man, Told was a sailor, and some fifty of the 135 pages of his book are devoted to recounting his adventures. The last thirty-four years of his life he occupied visiting prisoners in Newgate, especially those condemned to death, and exhorting them to repent. He tells us that during those years nothing remarkable occurred in either his "spiritual or temporal affairs," and therefore he confines himself for forty-eight pages to an account of his "researches into the situation of the prisoners at Newgate, and into the state of their souls." [47] This account consists largely of his recollections of the last hours of men and women whom he accompanied to the gallows. It has the same dismal fascination as those broadsides and pamphlets purporting to record the careers and dying speeches of famous criminals. The pages that directly concern his religious experience are really very few—no more than fifteen or twenty in all. Told's book has, as a consequence, a more general, if less intense, appeal than some others discussed here.

It may be that Told contemplated a more polite audience for his book than did, say, John Haime. He makes it clear from the outset that he considers himself to have fallen in the world. Both

---

the Unpardonable Sin," *Journal of Religion,* XXIII (1943), 115. "By . . . malicious, wilfull opposition to the strongest evidence of fact . . . and by their determined rejection of [Christ's] mission," the unconverted witnesses to the Crucifixion "committed the unpardonable sin." That sin, Newton insistently continues, is essentially "a deliberate and wilful refusal of the only means of salvation. It is the sign of final, absolute impenitence." Newton was, of course, not a Methodist; but Quinlan demonstrates that his view of the matter was a standard one to which most Christians subscribed.

his grandfather and father were successful physicians who lost their money in imprudent investments. Told still believes that he could reclaim a certain large and valuable piece of real estate—if only the witnesses were not all dead, if only the "writings" had not been stolen by a villainous housekeeper. He is proud of his ancestry, which he traces to Saxon times, and he records, with a mixture of pride and defiance, a bizarre tale on the order of Romulus, Remus, and the she-wolf to account for the original name of his mothers' family, Suckabitch, now changed to Sucksbury.[48] He is rather unpleasantly anxious to record any attentions that he has received from the gentry. He proudly recalls that three days a week the patroness of a village school that he taught "invited me with the curate of the parish to dine with her; and every other day, if I thought proper, to accompany the servants at their dinner in Knave's-Hall, as they termed it." [49] The prisoners who interested him most and with whom he had the strongest rapport were "all conspicuous characters in life."

> Mr. Brett was the son of an eminent divine in Dublin! Mr. Whalley a gentleman of a considerable fortune, and was possessed of three country seats of his own! Mr. Dupree was also the complete gentleman! and Mr. Morgan an officer on board one of his Majesty's ships of war! The last of these was frequently visited by Lady Elizabeth Hamilton (the Duke of Hamilton's daughter) both before and after sentence.[50]

To put it plainly, Told was a snob. This failing, however, adds to his book, contributing a touch of unconscious humor here and there without detracting from its intended merits. Told's early manhood was spent as an apprentice to the masters of several slave ships. He feelingly describes the horrors of that trade. Once, for example, to persuade a reluctant slave to eat, a Captain Tucker lashed him so savagely that "from his neck to his ancles, there was nothing to be seen but bloody wounds." This done, the captain repaired to his dinner table, which was laid in full view of the sufferer, "under the awning on the quarter-deck; he left the man . . . bleeding and groaning on the forecastle; came to his dinner like a hog, and eat without fear or shame." After his meal, the still-unsatisfied Tucker approached the slave again, this time armed with pistols. Pressing one against the man's forehead, he fired. The Negro "instantly clapped his hands to his head, one behind, and the other before, and stared the captain in the face, the blood gushing from his face like the tapping a cask, but he did not fall." It took two more shots to finish him, one to the ear and another to the heart.[51] In his years at sea, Told endured shipwreck, hurricanes, and capture by pirates, adventures that he spiritedly describes. But nothing equaled in strength the impression such scenes of cruelty made on him. One of his greatest blessings from God was the strength to quit the trade at a time when he was about to be "made a conspicuous character in that impious number of Guinea commanders," for he believed that as a captain he might "have proved as eminent a savage as the most notorious character among them." [52]

Though for a time a slave-trader, Told was always a pious one. In his years at sea, he was in an "unsettled state, sinning and repenting." [53] His conversion to Methodism in 1740 was not a conversion from unbelief, but a stirring-up of conscience to unremitting wakefulness. In his earliest childhood, "sister Dulcybella and self" used to wander "into the woods and fields, fixing ourselves under the hedges," and there converse "about God and happiness; so that at times I have been transported in such measure with heavenly bliss, that whether in the body or out of the body, I could not tell: this happiness attended me for a few years." [54] This joyous sense of the soul's uncertain tenancy of the body characterizes all of Told's most extreme religious experiences. Even the structure of the two such experiences he most fully describes is the same.

The first of these occurred when Told was twelve years old.

One afternoon, in the course of reading *Sherlock on Death,* he paused for a moment and, resting his right elbow on his right knee and supporting his head with his hand, meditated on "the awfulness of eternity."

> Suddenly I was struck with a hand on the top of my head, which affected my whole frame; the blow was immediately followed by a voice with these words, "Dark! dark! dark!" and although it alarmed me prodigiously, yet, upon the recovery, from so sudden a motion, I found myself broad awake in a world of sin. Notwithstanding all my former happiness and bliss, I now found a dreadful difference, as nothing could give me satisfaction, either from persons or things. . . .[55]

Soon afterward, though not the same day, he underwent a sequel to this distressing manifestation. Having nearly drowned in a swimming accident, he lay unconscious for three-quarters of an hour while his friends labored over him. Unaware of external things, he was vouchsafed during those minutes a "blissful vision." Told is cautious in recounting it, inviting our trust by admitting that his story "may appear rather incredible" though the events were "as real to my sensations" as, in the waking state, his sense of his own existence was.

> I rushingly emerged out of thick darkness into a most glorious city; the lustre of which . . . illuminated even the darkness, through which I seemed to urge my way, and enforced my entrance into that beatific state. . . . There was also some resemblance of a bottom or floor, like unto glass, but neither the city or bottom were of any substance. The inhabitants were all in the form of men, arrayed in robes of the finest quality, from their necks down to their feet; yet they also appeared to me of no material substance. What particularly courted my attention was, that not one of these celestial bodies were under any degree of labour to walk, as they all glided swiftly along, as if carried by the wind. This was my own case, clothed in the finest of linen,

> and conveyed with the like celerity. No speech or language was needful there, as they were all one soul.[56]

Such "solemn, sacred joy" as then he knew is impossible, Told believes, for anyone "in the body." The joy of liberation from the flesh consists in absolute freedom from that "world of sin" to which the divine hand and the warning exclamation "Dark! dark! dark!" had awakened him; in his vision he "had no imaginations of evil, or any temptations thereto, but was completely happy without mixture." [57]

The vision could not last, of course. Just as it reached a climax of perfection, it was withdrawn.

> [W]hile those blessed spirits were performing their aerial course, one of them about fifty yards off, on my right-hand, turned round, and looked steadfastly at my raiment: We both suddenly stopt, and the extacies which proceeded from his countenance united us together as one. Oh! who can express the sweet, pleasant, and serene tranquillity I then enjoyed! But, on a sudden, I lost all sense of this very desirable state, and clearly apprehended my being brought again into a sinful world; the coming into which was as through a devouring ocean of blood and fire.[58]

The union so highly valued in this passage seems almost sexual, and the benefit it confers, like one of the benefits of the sexual act, is release from the painful imprisonment in the self, a condition that Told associates with the "sinful world" into which he is thrust once more as he returns to consciousness through that "devouring ocean of blood and fire."

Years later, after his conversion to Methodism, Told once again underwent an experience of this sort. His vigorous faith had persisted for some time, but at length a period of trial and suffering succeeded, and Told became "clearly convinced of my unbelief, my lost estate, and of the carnal mind." His agony was so extreme that in the evenings, instead of going home to supper, he frequently took

> a solitary walk into the fields till nine, ten, and eleven o'clock, roaring for the frequent disquietude of my soul; and notwithstanding I could never accuse myself of inattention to any ordinance, fasting and praying, and sitting up both early and late, yet my unbelief prevailed, till I became completely miserable. In this situation I continued about three years, so that I "chose strangling rather than life"; nor could I, with all my hearing and self-denial, overcome this damning sin of disbelief.[59]

The "enemies of my soul," he tells us, suggested to him that, even if he should live five hundred years, he would "never receive a transformation of spirit by the grace of God." [60]

Such radical despair, the conviction that one has been specially excluded from grace, is a major theme in these autobiographies. Ostensibly, this sort of despair expresses the sufferer's sense of his absolute worthlessness. But we may speculate that the meaning of such a conviction is not quite as it is represented. It seems likely to me that, in his assertion of his uniqueness, the sufferer may sometimes be proclaiming at the same time the integrity of his self that refuses to submit finally to the sanctions of a religion that in its inclusiveness promises—or, as it appears to the self, threatens—salvation at the price of identity. Such a self prefers the painful distinction of standing outside the fold as the one lost sheep to the comforts of inclusion in the anonymous ninety and nine. The conviction that one is uniquely and irretrievably damned may be, in short, an act not of humility but of rebelliousness. Religion teaches us to regard such rebelliousness as sin; and so Bunyan, Told, and the others regard their despair, though not on quite these grounds. It is worth remarking that this despair, as it is the most extreme of the spiritual states into which these writers fall before they make peace with God, is often also the last—as though it constitutes the last-ditch stand of the ego.

Sometimes this crisis of despair follows on what the sufferer has conceived to be a happy conversion to religion, a complete and welcome submission of will and self to an encompassing power; in such cases, it reveals that conversion to have been only a truce, not a surrender. So it was with Silas Told; his conversion to Methodism was not secure. As he wandered through the streets and fields, Told wished himself to be each cow or dog he passed, considering it "ten thousand times happier" than he.[61] But at last one evening he was delivered—permanently, this time—from misery. Having secluded himself in a lonesome corner of a field, Told suddenly felt, as on that earlier occasion, a hand strike him on the head.

> I instantly found myself crying with a loud voice, "Praise God, praise God," and looking up, I beheld the ethereal universe, replete with the glory of God; and that glory of such substance and palpability, I thought I could have laid hold of it with my hand. This attended me for the space of a minute; but was succeeded by an uncommon thick darkness, through which a black dart, as if it was shot from the hill near Islington, pierced its way, and, with wonderful swiftness, entered my heart. I did not feel any pain thereby; but it was followed with these words, "This is one of your old delusions."[62]

The "this" seemed to Told cruelly ambiguous. Which was the delusion, the vision or his despair? He looked to heaven for a clarifying sign, and now, as he gazed upward,

> the heavens were unclosed about a mile in length, as it appeared to my mortal eyes, and tapered away to a point at each end. The centre of this awful and sacred avenue was about twelve feet wide, wherein I saw the Lord Jesus standing in the form of a man, holding both of his inestimably precious hands upright, and from the palms thereof the blood streaming down; floods of tears gushed from my eyes, and trickled down my cheeks. I said, "Lord, it is enough!"[63]

But there was more to come. At once "some articulate voice" asked:

"How did you find yourself an hour ago?" I then recollected that I was in a wretched and lost state. The voice again suggested, "All the world is but as one man, and one man as all the world." [64]

Like Woolman's and Haime's, Told's account is notably meticulous. The "black dart" is directed from "the hill near Islington." The rent in the heavens, "about a mile in length" and tapering "to a point at each end," is "about twelve feet wide." This is almost ludicrous. Yet Told's intention is plain; he means to convince us of the truth of his story by demonstrating that he was in possession of his senses at the time. He insists that the divine words he heard "were as clear to my intellectual sensations as the sun performing its diurnal course." [65] Told wants above all to be believed. Like the other religious autobiographers, he appears before us as a witness, and one whose credibility, as he well understands, he must take pains to establish. In the interests of that credibility, he insists that his experience, though entirely private, evinced a clarity of detail and a specificity characteristic of events and things whose reality no one denies.

But perhaps what is most remarkable in Told's account of this crisis in his religious life is the similarity between this event and the earlier one. Both times God announced himself by rapping Told on the head. This startling manifestation was succeeded by a vision in which Told was invited to pass out of himself—into union with a blessed spirit, in the first instance, and, in the second (as the voice proclaiming that "All the world is but as one man, and one man as all the world" suggests), into Christ. Both times Told is, in a manner, tempted to give himself up to something larger than he. On the first occasion, he could not. The vigorous, youthful self could not quite accede to its seducer. But on the second occasion, worn down by time and the entreaties of the will, his self gives up the struggle and its painful, precarious hold on its integrity.

I have been speaking of this sort of conversion, especially

when it involves the giving over of the melancholy distinction that attends the absolute despair that many of these religious men felt, as though it were a defeat. So it is, in a way—a defeat of self in a sense capable of a Christian interpretation. "In thy will is my peace." To those who undergo this experience, the defeat seems a happy deliverance. But it is good to understand what has been lost, for it is something that part of the man values highly. For certain sufferers—William Cowper is a notable example—the war is never entirely over. Again and again the self gathers its strength and returns to battle. And, even in those who appear to contrive a surrender, skirmishes sometimes remain to be fought. Thus Bunyan and Haime always had to fight the impulse to blaspheme in the pulpit.

For Silas Told, however, the surrender was final. The rest of his life was untroubled by doubt or spiritual malaise. One may speculate, to be sure, that his calling to minister to the condemned, his eager attendance on them to the gallows, and his careful observation of their behavior in their last moments express something dark in him. One may suppose that the scenes he witnessed were somehow associated in his mind with the terrible recollections of his years in the slave trade. Certainly Told spent a large part of his life in the presence of violent death. But he provides few clues to the meaning of this. Told's book reports on other things, and does so very well. It is an account, though one not entirely understood by its author, of the wars fought out in the spirit, those ambiguous struggles in which resistance sometimes seems defeat and surrender, victory. Of these matters, William Cowper's autobiography speaks even more clearly.

William Cowper and the Uses of Madness

William Cowper's *Memoir*, composed in 1766 though not published until 1816, is one of the earliest works of a man regarded as one of the most eminent poets of his time.* Biographers refer to it, of course; and so do critics, who find in Cowper's private distress, as it is recorded there, the source of certain of his poems. Seldom, however, does anyone treat the *Memoir* as a work in its own right, as a literary production with its own peculiar virtue, its own claim on our attention.

Donald Stauffer, to be sure, asserts that Cowper's work marks the accession of the genre of religious autobiography to the dignity of literature.[66] That judgment is perhaps too exclusive. Other books examined here can claim the respect that Stauffer pays to Cowper's. But Stauffer is right to value the *Memoir* highly. To be sure, Cowper's purpose did not differ from that of the other autobiographers with whom we have dealt: he wished to testify to God's mercy to him and to stir up in his readers a spir-

* Maurice J. Quinlan, ed., "Memoir of William Cowper: An Autobiography," *Proceedings of the American Philosophical Society*, XCVII (1953), 359–382. Hereafter, citations of this work will appear in parentheses in the text.

ituality as intense as his own. When, on the evidence of one who read it in manuscript, he came to believe that this book recorded experience too extraordinary to be useful to any public that he could imagine, Cowper determined not to print it (p. 363). His notion of its deficiency declares, in short, his conception of its purpose. But, though Cowper's intention was no more to create an aesthetic object than was, say, John Haime's, the man who was to become a poet produced a work expressing (in a good sense of the term) a literary sensibility. If Cowper's *Memoir* does not mark the debut of introspective autobiography as literature, it constitutes the debut of the literary person as an introspective autobiographer.

On the face of it, this distinction may seem an unnecessarily fine one. But it is not. It simply calls attention to the fact that the explicit literary exploitation of the inner life is something to which intellectuals came late. To private experience, and in particular to the experience of psychological distress, John Stuart Mill was to say, in a passage quoted earlier, his age owed "much both of its cheerful and its mournful wisdom." [67] My point here is that William Cowper was the first of what was to become the numerous class of intellectuals who recognized private experience to be a source of "wisdom" and that his autobiography, resembling as it does the works discussed in the three previous chapters, is evidence that he and those who came after him may owe this recognition in large part, both to certain heroes of religion and to a number of obscure, nearly anonymous, and markedly unintellectual persons.

The private experience in which Cowper deals is extreme experience—the experience of conversion, but conversion preceded and in fact determined by madness. More explicitly than his predecessors, he recognizes his mental crisis for what it was, a decline into absolute insanity. And, by both recognizing it and (in a complicated way) approving it, Cowper helps to begin the modern project of making available to serious attention abnormal states of mind, a project that for better or worse has vastly enlarged the scope of our moral and imaginative concerns.

One virtue of Cowper's book is its sharpness of focus. Like Bunyan and Haime, he leaves out of account nearly everything that does not bear directly on the main matter of his story: his passage through madness and despair to faith and relative (and temporary) serenity. The work is "a history of my heart, so far as religion has been its object," he says in the first paragraph (p. 366), and he is almost perfectly loyal to the formal principle here enunciated. He tells us little of his childhood—we wish that he told us more, for we suspect it to be more relevant than he imagined—but what he does record seems much to the point. One characteristic of Cowper implicated in his collapse was his extreme shyness, a dauntedness of spirit that prevented his appearing before any board of examiners or any body that could be conceived of as a court of judgment. An early expression of this timidity occurred when he was at school. There he became the favorite victim of a bully a few years older than he. So strongly did this boy's cruelty impress "dread of his figure" on Cowper's mind "that I well remember being afraid to lift up my eyes upon him higher than his knees" (p. 366). It may be that Cowper's later terror in the face of authority, a terror expressed in his frenzy at the prospect of examination before the House of Lords and in his recurrent conviction that he was mysteriously, irretrievably damned, had something to do with this early acquaintance with cruel and whimsical power. And the reader notices the economy and force with which Cowper renders his old fear: "I knew him by his shoe-buckles better than any other part of his dress," he writes (p. 366), a sentence that in the manner of a novelist enacts the emotion, rather than merely giving it a name.

Cowper records only a few more of his boyhood experiences. As a student at Westminster School, the most valuable instruction he received—most valuable because it was religious—occurred when, crossing a churchyard one night, he was attracted by a glimmering light. "Just as I arrived at the spot a grave-digger who was at work by the light of his lanthorn threw up a skull which struck me upon the leg." This reminder of mortality alarmed his conscience for a time, until, "surveying my activity and . . . observing the evenness of my pulse, I began to entertain with no small complacency a notion that perhaps I might never die!" (p. 367). The delusion did not last long. But in childhood this movement of Cowper's mind from one extreme to another anticipated the fluctuation of mood that was to plague him the rest of his life.

In 1749, Cowper, not quite eighteen, left Westminster, and early the next year he began the study of law. Three years later, he took up residence in the Middle Temple. Now, he says, "I became in a manner complete master of myself"—only to be plunged into the first of his periods of dejection (p. 368). "Day and night I was upon the rack, lying down in horror and rising up in despair." According to one trustworthy biographer, this period seems not to have been so absolutely gloomy as Cowper remembered it.[68] But there was good reason for the darkness of Cowper's recollection of this time. It was to conclude in what in his later madness he held to be his first commission of the unforgivable sin against the Holy Ghost.

For about a year, Cowper struggled with his melancholy. His pleasure in the classics disappeared as his distress deepened. The "uncouth" poems of Herbert were the only works in which he could find pleasure and comfort (p. 368). At last, urged by those anxious for him, he accompanied some friends to Southampton on a visit lasting several months. One morning early in their stay, the companions walked out to Freemantle, a place a mile or so from town:

> [T]he morning was clear and calm; the sun shone bright upon the sea; and the country on the borders of it was the most beautiful I had ever seen. We sat down upon an eminence at the end of the

> arm of the sea which runs between Southampton and the New Forest. Here it was that on a sudden, as if another sun had been kindled that instant in the heavens on purpose to dispel sorrow and vexation of spirit, I felt the weight of all my misery taken off; my heart became light and joyful in a moment; I could have wept with transport had I been alone (p. 368).

At that moment, Satan prompted him to believe that he owed his "deliverance to nothing but a change of scene and the amusing varieties of the place" (p. 368). He was to make a still worse mistake when, in 1763, in the depths of a worse despair, he recalled and condemned this "neglect to improve the mercies of God at Southampton" as constituting the unforgivable sin.

> No favourable construction of my conduct in that instance, no argument of my brother's who was now with me, nothing he could suggest in extenuation of my offences could gain a moment's admission. Satan furnished me so readily with weapons against myself that neither scripture nor reason could undeceive me (p. 376).

At the moment of writing, Cowper was no longer deceived. It was clear to his restored mind that on that morning near Southampton "nothing less than the Almighty fiat could have filled me with such inexpressible delight"; that day he had viewed a "flash" of God's "life-giving countenance" (p. 368). And, though he had sinned in misconstruing this manifestation, he had not sinned unforgivably. For the time being he understood, with Bunyan and others, that despair is itself a sin of the worst sort. Cowper's book, like Bunyan's, is in one of its aspects the account of his struggle to attain to that hopeful, sane, and profound judgment.

In the years just after his healing visit to Southampton, Cowper lived the life of a young man about town in London. His *Memoir*, keeping always to its announced theme, says little of this period. Cowper does not mention his unhappy attachment to his cousin Theodora; he does not mention his early literary efforts, among them translations of two satires of Horace and of part of Voltaire's *Henriade*. Nor does he allude directly to the Nonsense Club, though, when he speaks of his objections to hearing the gospel blasphemed (his only religious scruple at this time), he may well have in mind the conversation of that irreverent group.[69] By 1760, his patrimony was nearly spent. In 1763, providentially, as it seemed at the moment, a kinsman, a Major William Cowper, offered him the Clerkship of the Journals of the House of Lords. This offer he accepted, only to learn that he had "to expect an examination at the bar of the House touching my sufficiency for the post" (p. 370). The Lords were disturbed (with some reason, it seems)[70] at the Cowpers' management of their right of appointment to this and other clerkships and were investigating the matter; one step they took was to demand that young Cowper appear before them. "A thunderbolt would have been as welcome to me as this intelligence," Cowper writes. "They whose spirits are formed like mine to whom a public examination of themselves on any occasion is mortal poison may have some idea of the horrors of my situation; others can have none" (p. 370).

Now Cowper's severest trials began. To prepare for the examination, he had to visit the Clerk's office every day to study the manner of doing business there. But to no purpose. "Many months passed over me thus employed—constant in the use of means, despairing as to the issue" (p. 370). Again he tried a change of scene, the expedient that had served so well on that earlier occasion. At Margate this time, he recovered his spirits, though at first not completely. Each morning he awoke to the painful consciousness that the time of judgment was a day nearer. In these moments, he felt "like a man borne away by a rapid torrent into a stormy sea whence he sees no possibility of returning and where he knows he cannot subsist" (p. 371). But the pleasures of the day allayed his distress, and eventually he "acquired such a facility of turning away my thoughts from the ensuing crisis that for weeks together" he managed not to think of it at all (p. 371).

Reality was not permanently to be banished. In October, he returned to London, and now his terror was once more as fresh and total as at first. "I saw plainly that God alone could deliver me," he writes, "but was firmly persuaded that he would not and therefore omitted to ask it" (p. 371). Here Cowper formulates his plight without recourse to the theological phrases—"the unforgivable sin," "the sin against the Holy Ghost"—that he will soon employ. The naked plainness of this statement expresses, perhaps more vividly than those later ones in which language attempts to absorb Cowper's misery into some theory, the precise nature of the straits in which he finds himself; he is a man totally dependent on and totally hopeless of God's mercy.

In this state of mind, he "began to look upon madness as the only chance remaining" (p. 371). All along he had persevered partly out of unwillingness to embarrass his patron, and a mental collapse would provide that person, as well as Cowper himself, a legitimate reason for withdrawing. Now his main fear was that he would not go mad soon enough, and this fear suggested to him that he take his own life. The step from one to the other seemed easy. "Being reconciled to the apprehension of madness, I began to be reconciled to the apprehension of death" (p. 371). So extreme was his misery at the moment that the pains of Hell—if there were such a place—seemed "more supportable" (p. 372).

Still he vacillated. One morning in November, as he sat breakfasting in a coffeehouse, his eye fell on a letter in a newspaper. As Cowper remarks, it was perhaps at this moment (if such a moment can be specified) that his madness began in good earnest, for, the more attentively he read the letter, the more it "appeared demonstratively true that it was a libel or satire" on him.

> The author appeared to be acquainted with my purpose of self-destruction and to have written that letter on purpose to secure and hasten the execution of it. . . . I said within myself, "Your cruelty shall be gratified! you shall have your revenge," and flinging down the paper in a fit of strong passion I rushed hastily out of the room, directing my way towards the fields where I intended to find some house to die in, or, if not, determined to poison myself in a ditch when I should meet with one sufficiently retired (p. 372).

What followed was even more remarkable. Cowper's account of the next forty-eight hours of his life demonstrates, with unexampled clarity, the strength with which some healthy and resilient portion of a neurotic self may be able to oppose the destructive intentions of the conscious will. These pages in Cowper's memoir support Freud's notion, as stated in *The Psychopathology of Everyday Life*, that faulty and "chance actions" may be referred to "incompletely suppressed psychic material, which, although pushed away by consciousness, has nevertheless not been robbed of all capacity for expressing itself." [71] In Cowper, dark things were not repressed, but the wish in part of the self to remain alive.

It was forty-eight hours of warfare. Not long before, Cowper had bought half an ounce of laudanum, and it was with this that he proposed to poison himself. He had walked no more than a mile from the coffeehouse when it suddenly occurred to him that all he need do was escape immediately to France, where, becoming a Catholic, he might enter a monastery. Instantly he hurried home and began to pack. Now, just as suddenly, "self-murder was recommended to me once more in all its advantages" (p. 372). He quickly took a coach to Tower Wharf, where he planned to drown himself, and there he found the tide out and, as was to be expected, a watchman on duty "as if on purpose to prevent me" (p. 373). The purpose, of course, was not the watchman's but Cowper's.

Safe in the coach once more (the same one he had come in; apparently he had ordered it to wait), he thought of the laudanum again. Now he

> determined to drink it off directly; but God had otherwise ordained. A conflict that shook me to pieces suddenly took place—not properly a trembling but a convulsive agitation which deprived me in a manner of the use of my limbs, and my mind was as much shaken as my body (p. 373).

As he acutely remarks, he was "distracted between the desire of death and the dread of it"; even at the moment he "took notice of this circumstance with some surprise" (p. 373). Twenty times he attempted to drink, but he could not. He fared no better at home. Reaching for a basin into which he had poured the laudanum, he found that suddenly "the fingers of both hands were as closely contracted as if bound with a cord and became entirely useless." And now "the convincing Spirit" showed him the horror of what he had been about to do (p. 373). Hastily he poured out the laudanum. "This impulse having served, the present purpose was withdrawn" (p. 373); the instrument of death had vanished and, with it, for a moment once more, the desire to live.

Cowper spent the next day in bed in a state of "stupid insensibility," again determined to die but uncertain what manner of death to choose. That night he fell asleep for what he thought was to be the last time. "The next morning was to place me at the bar of the House, and I determined not to see it" (p. 374). At three he awoke and, taking his penknife into bed with him, lay "with it for some hours directly pointed against my heart. Twice or thrice I placed it upright under my left breast, leaning all my weight against it." Again he had contrived to frustrate his own will: "the point was broken off and would not penetrate" (p. 374).

He arose at seven. No time was to be lost, for his sponsor would soon arrive to take him to the House. Having bolted the door—he thought—he tied a garter into a noose and attempted to hang himself, once from a bedpost and once from the tester, both of which he broke. Now, almost successfully, he tried again, this time looping the garter over the angle of the door. There he dangled until at last, not surprisingly (but just in time), the garter parted and Cowper, unconscious now, fell to the floor. Regaining his senses, he went "reeling and staggering" back to bed. In a moment, much to his surprise, he heard his laundress moving about in the next room. It was she he had intended to keep out by bolting the door—a no-doubt-habitual operation that on this particular occasion he had managed not to perform. The woman sent for help, and soon his patron appeared to pronounce the welcome words, "My dear Mr. Cowper, you terrify me; to be sure you cannot hold the office at this rate—where is the deputation?" (pp. 364–375).

Cowper recognized as clearly as any modern reader the oddness of this chronicle.

> It would be strange should I omit to observe here how I was continually hurried away from such places as were most favourable to my design to others where it must be almost impossible to execute it—from the fields, where it was improbable that anything should happen to prevent me, to the Custom-house Quay, where every thing of that kind was to be expected; and this by a sudden impulse which lasted just long enough to call me back again to my chambers and was immediately withdrawn. Nothing ever appeared more feasible than the project of going to France till it had served its purpose, and then in an instant it appeared impracticable and absurd even to a degree of ridicule (p. 373).

Cowper ascribes the frustration of his attempts to God, "who alone had the right to dispose of" his life (p. 373). But Cowper's contradictory impulses and the series of "mistakes" he made are surely capable of the Freudian interpretation suggested earlier. Some part of him was determined not to let him destroy himself. The episodes that Cowper recounts may be described as a kind of battle in which two parts of himself struggle to achieve their opposite, deeply intended purposes.

But what if those purposes were really one? The struggle did achieve one purpose—the avoidance of the public test before the House of Lords. Perhaps the battle was a fiction, a drama staged by Cowper to excuse him to the world and to himself from the examination he so dreaded. The cessation of hostilities at the moment when the threat was withdrawn suggests as much; Cowper never meant to kill himself, but only to convince himself that he meant to do so. In this interpretation of the matter, those "faulty and chance actions" of the Freudian formulation are still seen to be at work—but in cooperation with their apparent enemy.

One may take still another view of the matter, a view including something of the first two. In suicide, according to the psychiatrist Karl A. Menninger, the desire to kill oneself is by no means always to be identified with the desire to die. In part of his mind, the suicide may simply wish to visit on himself, at the behest of inexorable conscience, the ultimate punishment, a wish to which another part of his mind, as victim, may be most unwilling to accede. The victim need not do active battle, for, though he does not wish to die, he may not desire very strongly to live. But he may evade his executioner as slyly as he can—as slyly as Cowper did. The interest of Menninger's notions is that they help us to understand why Cowper did what he did and why it should be an appearance before the House of Lords that occasioned so extreme a response. Further, they begin to explain the character of Cowper's later religious despair. For if, as Menninger maintains, the wish to kill oneself expresses "aggressive and punitive elements" in the psyche,* elements in the service of iron conscience, then, in the persons of the Lords and of his God, reality may have seemed to Cowper to be providing unbearably painful *simulacra* of a grim tableau already poised within him—on the one hand, hanging judge and executioner; on the other hand, a reluctant, uncooperative accused. This work of supererogation on the part of reality may have startled that interior court into action, as though circumstance had confirmed its rights.

But action to what end? Perhaps, as in Menninger's view, to procure the real death of the accused self in expiation of some crime against conscience, a punishment that the self regards, not as justified execution, but as self-murder (a term that Cowper uses several times). On the other hand, it may be that Cowper's strange behavior was a strategy that he devised to placate reality by taking upon himself (and contriving to thwart) the judicial office that circumstance was about to assume. Less dangerously, as it may have seemed to him, he could perform what reality threatened, magically and as though by ritual satisfying and forestalling it.

It is impossible to know which of these suppositions comes closest to the truth. But all of them proclaim one fact: what Cowper feared was judgment. He feared it, we may confidently infer, because he believed that it would discover in him a guilt he dared not contemplate. The nature of that guilt is forever obscure, to us as it was to him. But we may be certain that he felt it.† His

* Menninger himself mentions Cowper in this connection, though his knowledge of the *Memoir* seems to have been second-hand. Karl A. Menninger, *Man against Himself* (New York, 1938), pp. 72–74.

† At about this time, Cowper began to suffer—apparently only in imagination—from an obscure defect of his sexual organs. He seems to have thought himself a hermaphrodite. But, if he was, the fact would scarcely have gone unremarked by his schoolfellows and by the Templars, in whose company he had led a boldly masculine life for years. In *William Cowper of the Inner Temple, op. cit.*, pp. 143–144, Charles Ryskamp convincingly argues

notion that that letter in the newspaper was directed at him is evidence of this; it testifies to his fear of discovery—discovery of an intent to commit suicide in the first instance, but also a discovery actuated by the unnamed writer's desire to revenge himself on Cowper for some unspecified wrong. And Cowper felt that he had been appointed to that clerkship in the House of Lords partly as the result of an immoral desire. When his kinsman first suggested that he accept the post when the incumbent died, both men

> expressed an earnest wish for his death that I might be provided for. Thus did I covet what God had commanded me not to covet and involved myself in still deeper guilt by doing it in the spirit of a murderer. It pleased the Lord to give me my heart's desire and with it an immediate punishment for my crime (p. 359).

To the unconscious, the desire is the moral equivalent of the act, and this wish of Cowper's, though insufficient to explain all that followed, surely contributed to his distress. When the post was in fact offered, Cowper felt almost as he uttered the words of acceptance "a dagger at my heart" (p. 369). The shyness that had made such a job seem so desirable was now worse than ever: "a finger raised against me was more than I could stand against" (p. 370). At the office where he went through the motions of preparing himself for the examination, his feelings were "much like" those "of a man when he arrives at the place of execution" (p. 370).

---

that the defect was illusory, a "part of his mental disorder. . . . In acute cases of depression the subject is frequently unduly concerned about supposed changes in his body, and among these delusions sexual preoccupations are notable. These may be directed towards a particular organ, and, according to Fenichel, as a rule they represent in a distorted manner castration-anxiety." A delusion of this sort, involving fear of a shameful revelation, is consonant with Cowper's fear of an examination of any kind. His guilty secrets must not be disclosed.

In short, his notion that the letter in the newspaper was meant for him was only the most extreme and most nearly disastrous expression of his guilty self-consciousness. After his abortive attempt at suicide,

> I never went into the street but I thought the people stood and laughed at me and held me in contempt, and could hardly persuade myself but that the voice of conscience was loud enough for every one to hear it. They who knew me seemed to avoid me, and if they spoke to me seemed to do it in scorn. I bought a ballad of one who was singing it because I thought it was written on me (p. 376).

The words of chance acquaintances had once seemed to urge suicide; now all sorts of things—from Archbishop Tillotson's sermons to the plays of Beaumont and Fletcher—taught despair. "Everything preached to me, and everything preached the curse of the law" (p. 376).

"The curse of the law" is a phrase expressing the judicial aspect of Christianity. Cowper's attempted suicide had served to prevent his appearance before the Lords, but now it called him before the Lord God. His terror was absolute, as we shall see. But at least his deed had provided a sin for his baffled guiltiness to fix on. Here at last was an offense for which he could deserve to suffer. From the point of view of his psychic economy, it served a useful, if very painful, purpose, permitting him to evade the confrontation of whatever in his past had entailed his misery. Now his guilt had an object—an object nearly unbearable to contemplate, but, if these speculations are even approximately correct, preferable to the mysterious one that long had weighed so obscurely on his mind.

However useful his sin seemed to part of him, to Cowper's consciousness it was an immediate, relentless torture. He skulked through the streets, dining in taverns "where I went alone in the dark" and taking every care to hide from the accusing glance of his fellows. On these excursions, "I reeled and staggered like a drunken man; the eyes of man I could not bear; but when I thought that the eyes of God were upon me (which I felt assured of) it gave me the most intolerable anguish" (p. 376). Still, though he was "overwhelmed with despair," he had "not yet sunk into the bottom of the gulph" (p. 376). That "gulph" was, of course, the conviction that at Southampton years before he had refused God's grace, thereby committing the sin against the Holy Ghost that excluded him absolutely from salvation.

It scarcely needs to be argued that this passage in his autobiography is deeply felt. But *how* deeply felt is suggested by the imagery, which anticipates the concluding lines of "The Castaway," a poem Cowper wrote more than thirty years later in which he tells of a young sailor ("such a destin'd wretch as I") who is washed overboard and drowned.

> No voice divine the storm allay'd,
> No light propitious shone;
> When snatch'd from all effectual aid,
> We perish'd, each alone:
> But I beneath a rougher sea,
> And whelm'd in deeper gulphs than he.[72]

Into these depths he was to be cast several times. The occasion recorded in his *Memoir* was only the first—a fact that he could not know, of course, when he wrote it. But his recurrence in this late poem to the imagery of the early *Memoir* indicates that subsequent attacks revealed no greater horrors than did the first one.

In this state of mind, Cowper could sleep very little—only an hour some nights. Dreaming was more terrible than full consciousness.

> One morning as I lay between sleeping and waking I seemed to myself to be walking in Westminster Abbey, waiting till prayers should begin; presently I thought I heard the minister's voice and hastened towards the choir; just as I was upon the point of enter-

> ing, the iron gate under the organ was flung in my face with a jar that made the Abbey ring (p. 376).

Cowper tells us that, at the time of writing, he knew the interpretation this dream clearly invited to be a wrong one. He had come, like Bunyan, to believe that despair was not a response to sin but sin itself. To submit to it was to condemn one's soul to death, to commit spiritual suicide. At least it is as suicide that he seems to conceive of despair when he says, in a passage already quoted, "Satan furnished me so readily with weapons against myself that neither scripture nor reason could undeceive me" (p. 376). But, as he had thwarted and come to condemn his attempts at physical self-destruction, so at last was he empowered to resist its spiritual counterpart.

But not without the greatest difficulty. "Another time," he writes in a paragraph immediately following the description of his dream, "I seemed to pronounce to myself, 'Evil be thou my good.' I verily thought that I had adopted that hellish sentiment—it seemed to come so directly from my heart" (p. 376). This utterance is Satan's, and it appears in Book IV, line 110, of *Paradise Lost*, always one of Cowper's favorite poems. A little earlier, Cowper had called the temptation to despair "the capital engine in all the artillery of Satan," clearly an allusion to Milton's Book VI. There he associates himself with Satan's enemies, the embattled loyal angels. But, once his temptation has been accomplished, Cowper is Satan himself—and Satan in defiant mood. But more of Satan's speech than this concluding resolution seems relevant here. Satan has been reflecting on his sufferings.

> Which way I fly is Hell; myself am Hell;
> And in the lowest deep a lower deep
> Still threat'ning to devour me opens wide,
> To which the Hell I suffer seems a heav'n.*

* John Milton, *Paradise Lost,* Bk. IV, ll. 75–78, in *Complete Poems and*

Thus Cowper, to whom "life appeared . . . now more eligible than death only because it was a barrier between me and everlasting burnings." And Cowper is with Satan in inquiring,

> is there no place
> Left for Repentance, none for Pardon left?
> (11. 79–80)

The answer Satan gives himself we may believe to be Cowper's, too.

> None left but by submission; and that word
> *Disdain* forbids me. . . .
> (11. 81–82)

Cowper cannot admit the pridefulness of these lines to consciousness. But the phrase his heart supplied him, taken in its context, suggests that that quality of character was part of him.

> So farewell Hope, and with Hope farewell Fear,
> Farewell Remorse: all Good to me is lost;

Major Prose, ed. Merritt Y. Hughes (New York, 1957), p. 279. The citations that follow are to this edition and appear in parentheses in the text. The Satanic character of the unpardonable sin has already been suggested on pp. 133–134n., where John Newton's sermon on the subject is quoted. The essence of that sin is rejection and denial. Cowper could not in fact have been guilty of it, for the surest sign that one is innocent of it is concern about the matter. But Cowper thought differently. And, in his final period of depression years later, he once more associated himself with the Satan of *Paradise Lost:*

> Farewell, dear scenes, for ever closed to me,
> Oh, for what sorrows must I now exchange ye!
> Me miserable! how could I escape
> Infinite wrath and infinite despair!
> Whom Death, Earth, Heaven, and Hell consigned to ruin,
> Whose friend was God, but God swore not to aid me!
> ("Lines Written on a Window-shutter at Weston,"
> *Poetical Works* [London, 1926], p. 428)

Here, of course, God has rejected *him*. Like Satan, he takes a wrong view of the question.

> Evil be thou my Good; by thee at least
> Divided Empire with Heav'n's King I hold
> By thee, and more than half perhaps will reign. . . .
> (11. 108–112)

Here is more evidence for the assertion made in the previous section that the ultimate despair that some of these autobiographers experienced expressed, in part, a desire to maintain, at whatever cost, the integrity of the self against the including grace that self construes as a threat to its identity. "Better to reign in Hell than serve in Heav'n," says Satan at another point, and so, for a time, do these rebelliously despairing souls.

Like Satan, Cowper could not repent of his sins; he could only be tortured by them. But Cowper lacked Satan's spiritedness. A dryness of the spirit had come on him, that state of spiritual near-indifference of which others, from Bunyan to Mill, speak. "I knew that many persons had spoken of shedding tears for sin," Cowper writes, "but when I asked myself whether the time would ever come when I should weep for mine, it seemed to me that a stone might sooner do it" (p. 377). He was locked into that suit of iron armor of which George Whitefield spoke; the springs of feeling were inaccessible.* But one day, under the ministrations of his cousin Martin Madan, an Evangelical clergyman,

* Cowper explicitly associates this barrenness of soul with antipathy toward God in the second and third stanzas of "The Contrite Heart," one of his "Olney Hymns":

> I hear, but seem to hear in vain,
> Insensible as steel;
> If ought is felt, 'tis only pain,
> To find I cannot feel.
>
> I sometimes think myself inclin'd
> To love thee, if I could;
> But often feel another mind,
> Averse to all that's good.
> (*Poetical Works,* p. 438)

"those tears which I thought impossible burst forth freely" (p. 377). For a few hours, he was easier in mind. But that night he awoke from a short sleep to find himself in agonies of both mind and body. Here was the most extreme crisis of his disease. The pains of death and Hell alternated with a paralyzing numbness. "No convicted criminal ever feared death more or was more assured of dying," he says (p. 378), making the comparison of himself to a guilty man that by now we have come to expect. At noon the next day, his brother providentially at hand, Cowper fell into a state that clearly demanded professional attention. He recalls those moments vividly.

> While I traversed the apartment in the most horrible dismay of soul, expecting every moment that the earth would open her mouth and swallow me, my conscience scaring me, the avenger of blood pursuing me, and the city of refuge out of reach and out of sight, a strange and horrible darkness fell upon me. If it were possible that a heavy blow could light on the brain without touching the skull, such was the sensation I felt. I clapped my hand to my forehead and cried aloud through the pain it gave me. At every stroke my thoughts and expressions became more wild and incoherent; all that remained clear was the sense of sin and the expectation of punishment (p. 378).

Now Cowper was quickly placed in the charge of a Dr. Nathaniel Cotton, whose asylum in St. Albans had a good reputation which, by Cowper's account, it fully deserved. There he remained for eighteen months—from December, 1763, until June, 1765.

Of these, the first eight were the worst. All that happened during those months "may be classed under two heads—conviction of sin and despair of mercy" (p. 378). Cowper is more particular in another paragraph.

> A sense of self-loathing and abhorrence ran through all my insanity. Conviction of sin and expectation of instant judgement

> never left me. . . . The accuser of the brethren was ever busy with me night and day, bringing to my recollection in dreams the commission of long-forgotten sins and charging upon my conscience things of an indifferent nature as atrocious crimes (p. 378).

It is interesting to see in the last of these sentences his recollection and condemnation of his restless efforts to find in memory transgressions for which his present and anticipated sufferings might be said to answer. Once, as we have seen, his attempted suicide had been a sufficient object, but apparently it no longer served. Something in him seemed to hunger to find in the realities of the past occasions for his pain. Cowper came at last to recognize that this was wrong. He understood greediness of conscience to be a mental and spiritual disease. But it is worth noting that even this symptom of his madness was in a sense at the service of a crazy rationality. For what he sought to do was to balance the equation: if he suffered, it must be because of sin; otherwise the world made no moral sense. Misery he might be able to support, but not banality.

When five of those first eight months had passed, he found himself a little hardened to his condition.

> "Eat and drink for to-morrow thou shalt be in hell" was the maxim on which I proceeded. By this means, I entered into conversation with the Doctor, laughed at his stories, and told him some of my own, to match them—still, however, carrying a sentence of irrevocable doom in my heart (p. 378).

Now, slowly, he began to improve. Toward the end of the eighth month of his confinement, the "cloud of horror" withdrew (p. 378). "The Lord had enlarged my heart, and I ran in the way of his commandments" (p. 379). The transformation in his feelings is deliberately suggested by the substitution of "ran" for the "walked" of the passage to which he here alludes. Dr. Cotton feared, naturally enough, that this sudden transition might "terminate in a fatal frenzy," for "tears were ready to flow if I did but speak of the gospel or mention the name of Jesus" (p. 379). But, after nearly twelve months of probation, Cowper was pronounced cured; and now he retired to the village of Huntingdon, near Cambridge, where, by November, 1765, he was settled as a boarder with the Unwin family who for many years were to love and care for him. At this point, his *Memoir* ends.

The cure, I have said, was not permanent. Even at the time of writing, Cowper was still experiencing "many a lifeless and unhallowed hour." The happiness that he had achieved was only relative—"long intervals of darkness interrupted by short returns of peace and joy in believing." Still engaged "in a state of warfare" with Satan, he was subject to fits of anger (p. 380)—something new for him, he says, though its newness may in fact have been its direction against others rather than himself. But, for our purposes, the point is that he had attained a stability sufficient to allow him to contemplate and record his recent sufferings. The quality of his record, the phrases, sentences, and paragraphs I have quoted suggest this. Cowper searchingly confronts his recollections. His descriptions appear to issue from a desire to be rigorously exact, as though his report were subject to verification. Possibly there is something self-protective about this; by treating one's feelings like objects, one separates oneself from them a little. In any event, the record is remarkably and movingly clear.

Cowper stands with Bunyan, Fox, and Haime in having found language suitable to his occasions. But it is language of a different sort from theirs. As I said earlier, his book expresses a literary sensibility. Cowper's vividness is not Fox's. Cowper's style is not so starkly undecorated as his. Nor is Cowper's an oral style, as Fox's is, a style in which moments beautifully exist, but no larger movements or patterns. On occasion, Cowper can shape a sentence with almost the epigrammatic balance and force of Gibbon, though this is not his characteristic mode. The power of

Gibbon's style in his autobiography is largely its power to render culminations and summaries that perfectly and often poignantly communicate how Gibbon values the passage in his life that the immediately preceding paragraphs have lightly sketched. Cowper's genius is for rapid but controlled narrative, its details always relevant and (unlike those in Fox's book) always subordinated to the author's conception of the whole work.

Cowper shares this genius with Bunyan and such lesser autobiographers as Haime. But he differs from them, too, and once again his difference has to do with his more literary sensibility. Cowper's imagery is not drawn from the dumb circumstances of humble life. As a result, his book lacks some of the uncalculated and therefore even more moving pathos of Bunyan's and Haime's accounts, which find sermons in stones because there is nowhere else to look for them. But, if Cowper loses something, he gains something, too. His education and instinct enable him to draw more widely than these men on experience, not only of objects, but of the ideas and formulations of others. His allusions to Milton, for example, are not merely decorative. His reading had become a part of him, and his imagination had recourse to it in proposing to his consciousness the precise nature of his feelings. His literary experience, that is to say, had enlarged the vocabulary of his emotions, and it assisted him in representing his sufferings to himself and to us. Surely such flexibility and fluency in the naming and understanding of our feelings is one benefit we seek, however unconsciously, from literature. That benefit Cowper had received, and it leaves its mark on his book.

Control of the sort that Cowper exercises in his autobiography—control in the sense both of the formal coherence of the whole and of the deliberate clarity of particular formulations—is, as I have been suggesting all along, not merely an aesthetic but a moral concern. The deficiency of which I complained in Fox's work is that he shirks the task of inquiring of his experience what its principle of coherence is. No such charge may be brought against Cowper. As noted at the outset, he focuses sharply on "the history of my heart, so far as religion has been its object." And, further, like Bunyan, he insists on understanding his experience. Cowper, we have said, was terrified of judgment—but the judgment of others, not himself. Or, rather, in his sanity, he understands his fear of judgment to be the mark of madness. That understanding is a result of his willingness to enter at last into judgment on himself, to recognize, like Bunyan, that his hopelessness of grace was itself the sin to which it seemed to be a response. And, like Bunyan once again, Cowper insisted that the world make sense. Even in his madness he did this. His greediness of conscience, seeking in his past something to convict himself of, expresses several things, no doubt; but one of them is a horror at the apparent senselessness of his sufferings. The notion that he was irrevocably damned, painful though it was, was preferable; it permitted justice, of however harsh a sort, and, with justice, God to exist. I am suggesting among other things that Cowper's conviction that he was damned was, relatively speaking, a comfort to him. Once again, something in him had preserved him from the worst alternative that offered. His appetite for rationality, as instinctive as the desire of part of himself to resist execution, preserved enough of his moral nature to make recovery possible. And recovery took the form of ascribing to God's mercy a reality equal to that of his justice, a reality that, bringing good out of evil, was recompense for Cowper's pain and balanced the moral equation another way.

Or so we may read his story. This much is certain: like Bunyan's and those of some others, Cowper's autobiography may be described as an account of the attempt to wrest meaning from the experience of guilt. The passage from madness to sanity, from damnation to blessedness, is the passage from a wrong opinion to a right one about what that meaning is. These books make clear how mortally dangerous a journey it is. And hence these books declare their subjects to be heroes—heroes in a sense of the term easier for us to understand than for their contemporaries and themselves.

These chronicles of suffering are not chronicles of weakness. They detail crisis and collapse; but they end in victory, of however compromised, limited, and ambiguous a sort. Surely it is testimony to the essential strength of the self of a Cowper or a Bunyan—or a Haime or a Silas Told—that it insists on exploring the regions outside the fold of salvation, refusing the comforts (which at the same time it values and longs for) of faith which it fears will somehow annihilate it. This adventure in insanity is sin; but it is perhaps not a sin easy for us altogether to condemn. As Cowper testifies, it is a sin like Satan's, in which, from Cowper's lifetime to the present, many men have found everything to admire.

Perhaps it is not quite an accident that the Satanist view of *Paradise Lost* found its voice at the end of a century in which men had been exploring this dangerous territory. In any event, both the Satanists and some of these autobiographers in effect endowed madness—moral madness—with a positive value. Negation and denial were seen to issue from strength. To be sure, these autobiographers contrived to hide this fact from themselves. They do not quite discern that in some sense their sufferings are a credit to them, and in this there is a kind of modesty that adds to their attractiveness. Cowper's journey into Hell, as we have seen, appeared to him as a flight from a dreaded judgment. But it also had the positive aspect of a steadfast refusal of a part of himself to accede to injustice. His retreat into madness was, in one sense, an act of health; like the temporary paralysis of his hands as they clutched the vial of laudanum, it was the tactic by which the part of himself in love with life evaded a voracious conscience whose demands we may only call neurotic. A recognition of the deviousness and guile by which we serve ourselves is general now, and it is for this reason that I say we are better equipped than the writers and first readers of these autobiographies to recognize the heroism of these men whose strange experiences could only seem to them a mixture of curses and blessings manfully to be endured.

But, if what I have called the adventure in insanity is heroic, how can the return from it deserve, as I have said it does, the same praise? Is not this a retreat, and perhaps, since we have been admiring the advance so much, a blameworthy one? Perhaps the first thing to be said is that no man can live forever on the frontiers of experience. As even we who are relatively healthy-minded can testify, the faculties that protected Cowper's sanity by leading him into madness are sometimes strangely inefficient. We dream (we are told) so that we may sleep; but nightmares that wake us are a part of everyone's experience. So, too, the strategies intended to preserve the self may fail or go too far; Cowper's final attempt at suicide almost worked.

What I am suggesting here is that the strength of the adventurous, Satanic self, the strength that I have been praising, is not only the strength to make the journey but to *survive* it, to carry it through to some purpose. And that purpose is a man's daylight dealings with reality. The voyages out and back are one. And the return, one hopes, is not to the same condition from which one started, but to earned control, a new health. Here once more that sentence of Lionel Trilling's that I quoted in the chapter on Bunyan applies.

> Of the artist, we must say that whatever elements of neurosis he has in common with his fellow mortals, the one part of him that is healthy, by any conceivable definition of health, is that which gives him the power to conceive, to plan, to work, and to bring his work to a conclusion.[73]

The power to conceive, to plan, to work, and to bring a work to a conclusion is not the desire of the artist alone, but of every man.

That power, that health, is what a Bunyan or a Cowper achieved —achieved by surviving. It was incomplete power, to be sure. Cowper's journey had to be made again; Bunyan and Haime, as we saw, had always to repress the impulse to blaspheme rebelliously in the pulpit. But victory they did achieve, though a qualified one. And, in varying degrees of literalness, each of them might say, with William Cowper, that the madhouse was the place of his "second nativity" (p. 380).

IV

JAMES BOSWELL

The Book of Moments

James Boswell wrote memorandums, letters, an "inviolable plan," oaths, notes, journals, "papers apart"—but no autobiography. Nevertheless, to exclude Boswell from a study of English autobiography for that reason would be foolish, for in no writer, in English or perhaps any other language, has the autobiographical impulse expressed itself so vigorously and so voluminously. Boswell's interest in his states of mind, his insistence on cultivating in himself the feelings "proper" to a place or social situation, his sometimes-absurd "feudal" notions of family, his impulse to try on the personalities of the villainous and the obscure, his obsessive emulation of men possessing qualities he admires and lacks—all declare him to be a person who regards experience as *material*, material out of which the will may shape a life conceived of as a work of art. Boswell's intellectual and moral energies, that is to say, have in view an end that is partly aesthetic. What those energies were intended to produce was only incidentally the mass of autobiographical writings that (with *The Life of Johnson*) are the principal trace they have left behind; Boswell's object was a memorable life, a various but coherent self, comely and formed. But those papers testify to the pain and devotion that pursuit of such an object entails. They testify, too, to Boswell's kinship with the introspective Dissenters whose accounts of their lives have already been examined, for what I call here the aesthetic intention of Boswell's intercourse with experience is in effect a secular version of their attempts to shape and save their souls. And his kinship with many modern readers of his Journals,* whose longing for wholeness and health of mind resembles his for steadiness, cheerfulness, dignity, and consistency, is equally plain.

Boswell, then, has something to tell us about that shift in sensibility that, as I suggested previously, divides the nineteenth and twentieth centuries so sharply from preceding ages. The oddness of the manner in which we receive our knowledge of Boswell's uncomfortable, familiar self is evidence of this. If Boswell's Journals are not an autobiography, what are they? "Diary" is the most convenient term, and the distinction between a diary and an autobiography is an illuminating one. As Roy Pascal puts it, an autobiography is conventionally "a review of a life from a particular moment in time, while the diary, however reflective it may be, moves through a series of moments in time." [1]

One of Boswell's modern editors seems to have in mind such a movement through a series of moments in time when he speaks of the affinities that the Journals display for much twentieth-century writing. Boswell's appeal to us, Frank Brady suggests, has been

> prepared for by developments in contemporary literature. In his work, as in that of a novelist like Joyce, the major figures are delineated by a mass of apparently unselected detail, although the selection is actually controlled by Boswell's own range of perception and characteristic reactions.[2]

* When referring in my text to the body of Boswell's Journals, I shall merely capitalize without italicizing. A reference to a particular volume, however, will appear in normal form; for example, *The London Journal*.

More specifically, Boswell's Journals are, in the judgment of Northrop Frye, like the novels of Joyce again, an example of "literature as process," a mode in which emotion is kept "at a continuous present." [3] Frye opposes literature as process to literature as product, in which "suspense is thrown forward . . . and is based on our confidence that the author knows what is coming next." [4] In few works is emotion more consistently kept "at a continuous present" than in the Journals; in reading few works do we have less confidence that "the author knows what is coming next." Like *Clarissa*, Boswell's Journals are a book of moments.

In these respects, they differ as much from such a work as Gibbon's *Memoirs* as *Clarissa* does from *Tom Jones*, and differ in the same way. But the point of my comparison of *Clarissa* to the Journals is that Richardson was willing to diminish into an "editor" to achieve what Boswell provides almost without contrivance. This willingness on the part of an artist suggests that the effects to be gained thereby were very valuable to him. But valuable why? The answer may be that these effects, largely unavailable to literature conceived of as "product," answered best to his sense of how the world actually presents itself to the consciousness. It may be that part of what is new in a Boswell or a Richardson is a revised notion of reality, which, redirecting attention to psychic minutiae, works a transformation in sensibility—a transformation whose effects we still powerfully feel.

Frye and Brady suggest as much, however indirectly. To Frye, as we have seen, it appears that our experience of the representation of reality and, in particular, the reality of time, in twentieth-century fiction predisposes us to admire and enjoy certain eighteenth-century works in a way that might otherwise be impossible for us. To the importance of our notion of time as equipment for reading these earlier works, Ian Watt, in *The Rise of the Novel*, also testifies:

> The main problem in portraying the inner life is essentially one of the time-scale. The daily experience of the individual is composed of a ceaseless flow of thought, feeling and sensation; but most literary forms—biography and even autobiography for instance—tend to be of too gross a temporal mesh to retain its actuality; and so, for the most part, is memory. Yet it is this minute-by-minute content of consciousness which constitutes what the individual's personality really is, and dictates his relationship to others: it is only by contact with this consciousness that a reader can participate fully in the life of a fictional character.[5]

The *reductio ad absurdum* of this notion, when a novelist seizes on it, is exemplified in *Tristram Shandy*, where Sterne proposes to abolish the distinction between virtual and actual time, asserting (as Watt puts it) "a one-to-one correspondence between literature and reality" by "providing an hour's reading matter for every hour in the hero's waking life." [6]

These suggestions of Frye and Watt are interesting and useful. But they seem to rise from certain preconceptions that perhaps need revision. One notices immediately the confident tone of Watt's statement: nowadays we *know* what personality "really" is; it is the "minute-by-minute content of consciousness." In that knowledge, we are at last ready to understand Richardson properly. Together with Frye, Watt turns the matter on its head. He does not acknowledge that what is most important is not that our notions of what the reality of the inner life is ratify Richardson's and Boswell's, but that these and other eighteenth-century men were, in fact, discovering or inventing those notions that Watt and many of the rest of us still find engaging and satisfactory. That is to say, we do not enjoy *Clarissa* and Boswell's Journals because we enjoy *To the Lighthouse* and Molly Bloom's soliloquy. Quite the reverse; we enjoy Virginia Woolf and Joyce partly because we subscribe, by and large, to a conception of reality intuited and expressed by Richardson and Boswell and others two centuries ago.

Boswell is, then, one of the first to set down how it feels to live in the belief that, in point of reality, nothing exceeds the data of consciousness. As an abstract conception, this belief or something very like it is discernible in the works of Locke, Hume, and Berkeley. For Boswell, however, it is not a theory learned or intellectually arrived at; it is an unexamined supposition prior to thought. Boswell's unfixed mind often sought occasions to distress itself with clumsy philosophical doubts. "I felt myself in a sort of wild state of mind, metaphysical and fanciful, looking on the various operations of human life as machinery, or I could not well describe what," he says at one point, an utterance whose conclusion, trailing off into inconsequence as it does, typifies the ineptitude of most of his abstract speculations.[7] But never did Boswell question the reality and value of the data of consciousness.

> No matter what; I am pleased and want no more. I know it is against principle; I know [what] Lord Kames and other cool analysers of feeling could tell me. . . . But I cannot feel by reason, and therefore, when an object excites pleasure in me, I call it pleasing, be it a dance at Sadler's Wells, a ballad sung by porters against the ministry, a roasted apple from a stand at Temple Bar, a Methodist sermon, or a print of the world turned upside down.[8]

Consciousness was not always so pleasing, of course. "What misery does a man of sensibility suffer!" [9] Boswell exclaims. But "as I would not wish to have my body of stone, so I would not wish to have my mind insensible." [10] Indeed, "there is a pleasure in being to a certain degree agitated by events"—a pleasure, that is, in the sense of one's own existence.[11]

The intimate connection between Boswell's fascination with the series of his ideas and feelings and his style and narrative method remains to be demonstrated, a task that requires us to examine particular phrases and sentences, particular journal entries, and particular sequences of events as set down in his record. It is not my business here to consider, as others have done, the Journals as the raw materials of *The Life of Johnson*. Reading the Journals we realize—"with a shock," an editor has remarked —that each familiar scene of the *Life* is "a fragment of Boswell's autobiography torn loose from its context." [12] That shock is salutary, I believe, for it dramatizes the autonomy of Boswell's Journals as opposed to the *Life*, the prior interest of what is, in a sense, the greater work.

To be sure, it is instructive to watch the final form of a passage in the *Life* evolve from a memorandum or a journal entry. (And this is also true of the earlier *Tour to the Hebrides.*) [13] As the incident moves from the obscurity of recollection and private record toward the light of print, Boswell's private peculiarities recede. We do not have Johnson on Boswell, but Johnson on a Subject; and we have him increasingly in focus, increasingly *present.*

On the other hand, just *where* he is, is not clear. Boswell's best moments, in the Journals and in the *Life*, are never his descriptions of physical objects. Boswell was quite aware of this deficiency. "In description we omit insensibly many little touches which give life to objects," he says. "With how small a speck does a painter give life to an eye!" [14] Landscapes reduce him to cliché; he can think of nothing fresher to say of the Alps than that they are "horridly grand." [15] He is more capable than he imagines, however, of that speck that gives life to an eye. Persons and encounters, especially, he can quicken by suggesting his response to them. Lady Margaret Hume, "a woman pretty clever, but snappish," [16] lives in memory, as does a certain French merchant, "young, pock-pitted, and repeating sentences as if he had got them by heart." [17]

In each case, the person and Boswell's response to them appear before us simultaneously. Indeed, the person tends to disappear into the response, though not so absolutely as do the Alps in his "description" of them. But, in Boswell's account of the occasion when a "little, short, thick-legged, sniveling urchin" stood "shaking himself and rubbing his pockets, while Johnson rolled superb," the persons and actions and Boswell's response to them compose a fully realized scene.[18] On the one hand is the boy; his shortness and Boswell's contempt for him are communicated, first of all, by the doubling of the adjectives that describe his size. Literally and figuratively, Boswell is looking down on him; he ignores the face, where a person's identity and therefore his dignity are most clearly displayed, except in an adjective of disgust, "sniveling." On the other hand is Johnson, whose comportment is as grotesque as the boy's, but not ridiculous. Boswell does not paint the streaks of this tulip. The whole familiar figure of "majestick" Johnson looms above the boy; he "rolled," but rolled "superb." Boswell's vigorous verbs and adjectives set off the contemptibly particular against the nobly general. Here is Gulliver in Lilliput—a physical and moral confrontation of the tiny with the great. The point is that the meaning of this little drama would not be so apparent had Boswell reported it dispassionately. Boswell's art centers in himself. The world is real insofar as he responds to it.

Boswell's responses were not, of course, always interpretive. Often he was willing to rest with mere perception. An example chosen almost at random is his account of an evening when, "low-spirited and melancholy," he abandoned his friends and, "mounting on the back of a hackney coach, rattled away to town in the attitude of a footman. The whimsical oddity of this, the jolting of the machine, and the soft breeze of the evening made me very well again." [19] Here the incongruous elements of the experience—his awareness of his own oddity, the noise and discomfort of the journey, the pleasant summer air—are simply set down. No conclusion is drawn; no judgment is made. The experience does not *mean;* it merely *is*. It consists of elements whose only unity is their simultaneous presence in the consciousness of James Boswell at a certain hour on the night of June 27, 1763. Boswell's assertion in such passages—and there are many of them—of the parallelism, in his own mind, of perceptions that differ considerably in character and degree of abstraction resembles strikingly the example that Fowler gives of "syllepsis": "Miss Bolo went home in a flood of tears and a sedan chair." Indeed, it might almost be said that, for Boswell, something like syllepsis is a characteristic mode of experience.

Boswell is, then, capable of perceiving and setting down in a sentence or two those sometimes-discordant elements of consciousness that are simultaneously present to his mind. Naturally enough, a *succession* of moments (that "minute-by-minute content of consciousness" of which Watt speaks) is likely to require more space to record. For example, in the Journal covering his London jaunt of 1776, he describes an occasion when a Mrs. Cholmondeley, Sir Joshua Reynolds, and he discussed "drawings of the mode of burying the dead in Otaheite." While they

> looked at these mementoes of mortality, a kind of pleasantry was bandied between Mrs. Cholmondeley and Sir Joshua about "this sad thing death," and the Knight in particular was quite delicate and fine and smiling while he talked of it. I could not help steadfastly thinking, how strange is it that these two, who are themselves certainly to die, should even for a few moments treat the awful and tremendous destruction of this scene of existence with such levity. The thought grew full and solemn at once.—And then my mind made a transition to something else.[20]

Here Boswell records his sense of the incongruity between the matter of the conversation and Sir Joshua's manner—"delicate and fine and smiling"—and of the train of reflections that incongruity provokes in him. That his ideas are uncomfortable is perhaps suggested by his saying that he "could not help" conceiving them. But the fact is—and it fascinates Boswell—that his reflections have a life of their own and grow "full and solemn at once." At last, with a comic effect of which Boswell seems aware, "—And then my mind made a transition to something else." What that something else was Boswell does not say. The focus here is on the sequence itself, on the ability of a set of mixed impressions to initiate a train of sober thought which in turn is suddenly and inexplicably replaced by another (and by implication trivial) datum of consciousness. Similarly, in the entry marking his departure from Turin in 1765, he writes,

> I sent to Mme. S——— and begged she would return me my letter. She bid the valet say that she had thrown it in the fire. Here was the extreme of mortification for me. I was quite sunk. . . .
>
> I set out at eleven. As I went out at one of the ports, I saw a crowd running to the execution of a thief. I jumped out of my chaise and went close to the gallows. The criminal stood on a ladder, and a priest held a crucifix before his face. He was tossed over, and hung with his face uncovered, which was hideous. I stood fixed in attention to this spectacle, thinking that the feelings of horror might destroy those of chagrin. But so thoroughly was my mind possessed by the feverish agitation that I did not feel in the smallest degree from the execution. The hangman put his feet on the criminal's head and neck and had him strangled in a minute. I then went into a church and kneeled with great devotion before an altar splendidly lighted up.[21]

Here Boswell pays more attention to the content of the sequence and its usefulness to him; he rushes to the execution in the hope that "the feelings of horror might destroy those of chagrin." But clearly he is also fascinated simply by the variety of feelings that press on the heels of one another. "Here then I felt three successive scenes," he continues; "raging love—gloomy horror—grand devotion." And he is disappointed (and morally uneasy) when he reflects that, in fact, the series was not so complete as the occasion suggested it might have been: "The horror indeed," he writes, concluding the episode, "I only *should* have felt." [22]

Such a succession of states of mind frequently dominates an entire entry, though the moments recorded comprise no more than a fraction of the day. An absolutely complete record is impossiblc, of course, for

> the variations within, the workings of reason and passion, and, what perhaps influence happiness most, the colourings of fancy, are too fleeting to be recorded. In short, so it is that I defy any man to write down anything like a perfect account of what he has been conscious during one day in his life, if in any degree of spirits.[23]

The attempt would, indeed, involve him in Shandean absurdity. Obviously enough, not *every* impression, feeling, or idea is set down in even the most rigorously minute of Boswell's narratives.

Principles of selection, then, were necessary. Faithfulness to the temporal sequence of leading impressions is, as we have seen, one such principle; another, and one just as capable of imparting that impression of a "continuous present" so characteristic of the Journals, is the setting cheek by jowl of ideas, feelings, or observations that may not have occurred absolutely in series, but are thematically associated with one another in Boswell's mind. Thus, of one evening of his pilgrimage to Lichfield, Boswell writes,

> I talked to [Johnson] of Dr. Boswell's going to bawdy-houses and talking as if the Christian religion had not prescribed any fixed rules for intercouse between the sexes. He said, "Sir, there is no trusting to that crazy piety." I was humbled by this strong saying. After dinner I had visited his house. A beautiful, gentle, sweet maid showed it. In one of the garret rooms I kissed her, and she curtsied. I was charmed with her for the moment as with a rose or some pleasing object which makes a slight but very vivid impression.[24]

Boswell is charmed, and so, it seems likely, are his readers. The impulse to kiss a girl in sober Johnson's house expresses Boswell's willingness (to be examined more closely later) to assist the world in supplying him with curious, contrary sensations. And his language neatly renders the delicate momentary impression she made on him. But of course this is not all there is to the paragraph. The first half contains an exchange between Boswell and Johnson, innocent enough out of context, on right religion and sexual conduct. Clearly, this conversation is not so academic as Boswell would have Johnson believe; the two halves of the paragraph are thematically related. And, as the tense of the transitional sentence indicates ("After dinner I had visited his house."), the kiss in the garret was given before the conversation occurred and probably gave rise to it.

Two kinds of sequence are suggested here. On the one hand, there is the order of events as they actually occurred; but Boswell plays this down. On the other hand, there is the order of Boswell's ideas at the time that he came to write his Journal—the order that this entry represents.* In addition, then, to actual time, actual sequence, we sometimes find in Boswell another temporal dimension, which we may call "Journal time." What Frye says of *Tristram Shandy* is true of the Journals: "[W]e not only read the book but watch the author at work writing it. . . . [W]e are not being led into a story, but into the process of writing a story. . . ." [25]

Essentially, of course, this distinction between actual time and Journal time is not so real as at first it may seem, for recollection is itself an event that one may wish to record. When Boswell reverses or otherwise alters the actual sequence of events, he is

* In his introduction to *The London Journal*, Frederick A. Pottle warns us that we should "remember that Boswell did not write his journal in daily installments as the events occurred. He would sometimes fall days behind and then catch up at a sitting" (p. 12)—usually working from brief memorandums set down on the day in question.

not in fact recording the past but the present, the moment of writing. Considered in that light, Journal time is just as "actual" as other portions of the record. One point of these observations is that, when he writes in this fashion, Boswell is vaguely and accidentally expressing a conception of autobiographical writing that, as we saw in the earlier dicsussion of *The Prelude*, was to become important to Wordsworth, as in a rather different sense it had been to Bunyan. This notion was that the act of recollection may itself be as important an experience as any event recollected, the notion that autobiography, in Roy Pascal's words, is "not simply the narrative of the voyage, but also the voyage itself." [26] Boswell does not move far in that direction. His self-recording does not really help him understand much. But such displacements of events as sometimes occur in his journalizing, such superimpositions of Journal time on actual time, do manage, however accidentally, to reveal or simply to emphasize the more nearly permanent preoccupations of his mind, its patterns of association.

The main point here is not so much that the principle of selection and organization in a Boswellian paragraph may be what I have called Journal time as that it need *not* be actual time, in the simplest acceptance of that phrase. And, when it is not, a theme is often being suggested, an associative chord sounded. Thus, in four words, an entire entry from the period when Boswell, combating drunkenness, struggled in narrow and narrowing circumstances to complete his biography of Johnson, he expresses the barrenness and urgency of those days: "*Monday 23 April.* Only Water. Some *Life*." [27] But he expresses it indirectly, implying, by silence, the exclusive importance of labor and sobriety and, by their juxtaposition, the grim dependence of one on the other. To repeat, though actual time often determines the shape and character of a particular Journal entry, it need not always do so. And further, the sense of the essential unity of a passage in Boswell's life that we sometimes derive from larger sections of the Journals is owing not so much to his loyalty to actual time as to his relentless preoccupation with an idea, a person, or a feeling. That is to say that the unity of such portions of the Journals is thematic.

That paragraph about the kiss in the garret and the conversation about sexual morality provides a clue to one such theme. There in miniature is recorded one of Boswell's dominant preoccupations during his 1776 jaunt to London—"dalliance" and the desire to be absolved of guilt about his sexual irregularities. These matters were on his mind in Edinburgh, too. But in London, the home both of available women and of Dr. Johnson, they became increasingly important. The "brutal fever," accompanied now by drunkenness and fits of violence, was stronger in him than it had been for years, but his conscience was still active, if only intermittently. The problem was, as his editors put it, that for Boswell "words were everything. Promiscuity, if called by its right name, had an ugly sound, but concubinage was biblical and 'Asiatic,'" and therefore—perhaps?—excusable.[28] It was a vexing question, and one on which Boswell foolishly hoped Johnson would be willing to give a permissive opinion. Thoughts of this sort arose even when he was "warmly pious." "Nothing disturbed me," he says of one such occasion,

> but a degree of unsettledness as to the consistency of concubinage, or rather occasional transient connexions with loose women, and Christian morals. I was sensible that there was a great weight of interpretation against such license. But as I did not see precisely a general doctrine for practice in that respect in the New Testament, and some Christians, even Luther, did not think it an indispensable duty to cohabit only with one woman, and my appetite that way was naturally strong and perhaps rendered stronger by encouragement, I could not decide against it. I *must* venture to consult Dr. Johnson upon it.[29]

The tone of that last sentence communicates Boswell's accurate perception that the project was a dangerous one. It took him some time to work up his courage. In the meantime, he consorted with whores—six times in four consecutive days, in one "rage." [30] Again and again, as in that conversation at Lichfield, he tried to get Johnson's approving counsel. "I mentioned the licensed stews at Rome. . . . I urged the common topic that whores were necessary to prevent the violent effects of lewdness, and prevent our wives and daughters from being ravished." [31] On Easter, in a dangerously more personal way, Boswell asked "whether a man who had been guilty of vicious irregularity would do well to force himself into solitude and sadness." [32] And then follows a gap of two days in the manuscript, days during which, the editors surmise,

> it would seem that Boswell had done or said something that offended Johnson to an unusual degree. . . . Perhaps he finally reached the stage of a confession and was severely scolded. Or possibly Johnson simply got tired of the tone which the conversation, under Boswell's leading, seemed always to be acquiring, and told him that he had had enough of it.[33]

In short, the concerns that animate a paragraph or an entry may, if they are strong, impart a sense of unity to a body of Journal. We should not suppose, however, that this was always or even usually the result of art. After all, as a truthful diarist, Boswell is finally the prisoner of his experience. He must record his preoccupations, and, if he has had only one, the reasons for its prominence in his pages are not far to seek. But on certain occasions he achieves the effect of unity deliberately. Of such conscious calculation of means and ends the early *London Journal* for 1762–1763 provides the best example.

It does so for an interesting reason. In later years, Boswell would go to considerable lengths to ensure the privacy of his record. On occasion, for example, in the vain hope that one of his escapades might thereby escape his wife's knowledge, he took the trouble to transliterate some entries into Greek characters.[34] But the early *London Journal*, unlike the others, was intended for an audience—his friend John Johnston, to whom he posted it in installments. It was an audience of one, to be sure, but an audience still. And he wished to entertain that audience. Hence the planned effects, achieved seemingly without effort; hence the artfully contrived suspense and unity of particular episodes. Of these episodes, the affair with Louisa is, as every reader will acknowledge, the most striking.

It is a comedy, of course—the comedy of a man who, to avoid risking the pain and expense of gonorrhea, attaches himself to a girl whom he considers safe, only to contract a bad case of that disease from her. The act begins on a note of middle-class high refinement: " 'And pray,' said she, 'when shall I have the pleasure of your company at tea?' " Their style is always thus elevated.

"Madam, . . . from the first time I saw you, I admired you."

"O, Sir."

"I did, indeed. What I like beyond everything is an agreeable female companion, where I can be at home and have tea and genteel conversation." [35] These snug comforts were not, of course, his only objects. Nor were they Louisa's. Boswell, she knows, is not in a position to take her into keeping, but she feels that she owes it to herself to get something from him, if only as a kind of commitment, an earnest of his future generosity. "I am in a bad humour this morning," she says on one occasion. "There was a person who professed the greatest friendship for me; I now applied for their assistance, but was shifted. It was such a trifle that I am sure they could have granted it." Boswell does not remark on, though he notices clearly enough to record, Louisa's equivocations as to the sex of this friend. One contract has been terminated, and another is being very delicately proposed. Louisa is hinting that Boswell pay her "trifling debt," the sum of which she tantalizingly refuses to specify. "I was a little confounded and embarrassed here," Boswell writes. "I dreaded bringing myself into a scrape. I did not know what she might call a trifling sum. I have resolved to say no more." But he ventures. " 'Pray, Madam, what was the sum?' 'Only two guineas, Sir.' Amazed and pleased, I pulled out my purse." Boswell is willing to accept her moderate demands; but the time has come to define the terms of his future contractual obligations: "Madam!" he exclaims, "though I have little, yet as far as ten guineas, you may apply to me." The agreement has been signed, and there only remains the plan for carrying it into execution. " 'But when may I wait upon you? Tomorrow evening?'. . . . 'What? to drink a dish of tea, Sir?' 'No, no, not to drink a dish of tea.' (Here I looked sheepish.) . . . I kissed her again, and went away highly pleased with the thoughts of the affair being settled." [36]

Neither party is deceived. "I would live upon nothing to serve one that I regarded," Boswell grandly concludes at the very moment that he is thinking: "[M]y naming the sum of ten guineas was rash; however, . . . it cost me as much to be cured of what I contracted from a whore, and . . . ten guineas [is] but a moderate expense for women during the winter." [37] This comedy of contrasts continues in incident after incident. One Sunday, taking advantage of the household's absence at church, Boswell was

> just making a triumphal entry when we heard her landlady coming up. "O Fortune why did it happen thus?" would have been the exclamation of a Roman bard. We were stopped most suddenly and cruelly from the fruition of each other. She ran out and stopped the landlady from coming up. Then returned to me in the dining-room. We fell into each other's arms, sighing and panting, "O dear, how hard this is." "O Madam, see what you can contrive for me." "Lord, Sir, I am so frightened."
>
> Her brother then came in. I recollected that I had been at no place of worship today. I begged pardon for a little and went to

> Covent Garden Church, where there is evening service between five and six.[38]

And when, at last, they do enjoy a "paradisial" night together, the final ground for self-congratulation, the circumstance that climaxes the lyric description of his sexual athleticism, is Boswell's comfortable observation that "[T]he whole expense was just eighteen shillings." [39]

Six days later, he perceived the first signs of his infection. Two days after that, his suspicion confirmed, Boswell, very much on his dignity, conducted a final, reproachful interview with her. He writes ruefully:

> Thus ended my intrigue with the fair Louisa, which I flattered myself so much with, and from which I expected at least a winter's safe copulation. It is indeed very hard. I cannot say, like young fellows who get themselves clapped in a bawdy-house, that I will take better care again. For I really did take care.[40]

Thus ends the comedy, in ironic reversal and chagrin.

As one critic has suggested, in this episode Boswell has so carefully arranged his narrative that actual events almost assume the form of a fiction.[41] Here is an instance of a Boswellian impulse that we shall examine shortly—the impulse to conceive of life, or a passage in a life, as a work of art. The point at issue here is, however, different. What I suggested earlier, that Boswell's Journals are examples of literature as process because he necessarily cannot know what is coming next, is not everywhere true or not true only for that reason. Often, as in the Louisa episode, he *does* know a little of the future, for he posts his Journal a week or so at a time. It is likely, for instance, that the account of his joyful night with Louisa was composed on the day that he discovered that she had infected him.[42] By then, of course, the affair was all but over; but Boswell does not permit that later knowledge to intrude on his record of the past. He is constantly and consciously true to the event as it was. Boswell's deliberate efforts to compel the moment to exist in his pages, no matter how foolish or wrong the record of it may later show him to have been, asserts his intuition of the dignity of the fleeting data of consciousness as the prime, irreducible elements of reality.

In Boswell, at least to a degree, the very sprawl and variety of the documents are a part of the meaning. Boswell never rose to such an abstraction, nor did he ever try to do so. But surely it is the genius of his Journals that, in phrases, sentences, paragraphs, whole entries, and even in larger movements of the narrative, he manages, sometimes by accident and sometimes by will, to express so coherent a view of things. There is almost a paradox here, for this coherent view is essentially a view of incoherence, an equation of the reality of a man's total experience with the sum of appearances as, one by one, they present themselves to his consciousness. I have said that Boswell's is a book of moments—millions of them. It is impossible to speak intelligibly of the form of such a work. It has no form, and yet, again almost paradoxically, this deficiency itself has one of the effects that we have been taught to admire in the willed order of the shapeliest productions of art; here if anywhere, manner and matter are one.

Being Boswell

No one reads Boswell's Journals to determine what his notion of reality was. Many modern readers share that notion with him, a fact that partly accounts for our openness to his revelations. When our interest in Boswell's Journals is not interest in the origins of *The Life of Johnson* or in eighteenth-century life and manners, but in Boswell himself, it is, I suggest, very largely a function of our interest in ourselves.

To say this is not precisely to praise ourselves. It is not Boswell's genius that we share with him. "In a sense," W. H. Auden wrote in a review of the *London Journal*,

> Boswell triumphs as a writer because in all other respects he is such a thoroughly ordinary man. He is not clever; he never astonishes us with an observation we could not have had the insight to make; he is not abnormal; his feelings and behavior are never such that we cannot easily imagine ourselves feeling and doing the same. Consequently, in reading Boswell each of us is confronted by himself.[43]

Auden is not entirely right. Boswell *is* clever—from time to time, at least; now and again his insight *does* astonish. But surely the essential point is well taken. The question is, with what in ourselves does Boswell confront us?

The answers to this question are no doubt as many and as

various as are Boswell's responsive readers. Like many of us, Boswell is a moralizing sensualist, gauche, absurd, ambitious, feckless, and occasionally admirable. But there is nothing peculiarly "modern" here. "All is human," as the Beggar in Gay's opera says. However, there is more to it than this. Boswell's almost obsessive concern with certain subjects is an expression of anxiety and insecurity; and these conditions of mind (as the passage of the terms into the vague vocabulary of modern cant testifies) are held by many—rightly, I think—to characterize the present age.

Boswell's very habit of journalizing is evidence of his anxiety and insecurity, or so the various reasons he gives for this activity suggest. One of the reasons is, to be sure, very practical, very obvious. What he calls "bottled" conversations[44] are a staple of the Journals, which were intended to be a repository of anecdote. "I take pleasure in recording every little circumstance about so great a man as Mr. Johnson," he writes early in their acquaintance, for each "little specimen . . . will serve me to tell as an agreeable story to literary people." [45] Here is the germ of the *Life*. From the first, the Journals were to be put to some worldly use, and in a manner he can define. As he accurately and happily noted: "A page of my Journal is like a cake of portable soup. A little may be diffused into a considerable portion." [46]

But his record also has more private uses. It is the "faithful register of my variations of mind" [47]—variations that always fascinated him, however painful they might be. Moreover, it was itself an occasion of such variations. It serves as a "reservoir," that is, a source, of ideas.

> According to the humour which I am in when I read it, I judge of my past adventures, and not from what is really recorded. . . . If I am in gay spirits, I read an account of so much experience, and I think, "Sure I have been very happy." If I am gloomy, I think, "Sure I have passed much uneasy time, or at best, much insipid time." Thus I think without regard to the real fact as written.[48]

Reading of his experience is a valuable experience itself. Even the record of so generally unhappy a period as the Edinburgh winter of 1775–1776 can cause him pleasure, though it raises for a moment the supposition "that if I keep in constant remembrance the thoughts of my heart and imaginations of my fancy, there will be a sameness produced, and my mind will not have free scope for alteration." The manifest improbability of such a result at once occurs to him, and he comfortably concludes that "one new idea or former one revived will introduce a group." [49] The Journals stimulate recollection and hence vivid consciousness, renewing his sense of life.

They were valuable to him, not only in the reading, but also in the writing, especially as an alleviation of the pains of melancholy to which he was often subject. "Could I extract the hypochondria from my mind," he says at one dark moment, "and deposit it in my journal, writing down would be very valuable." [50] The implication of this sentence is that he *cannot* thus "extract the hypochondria"; he cannot purge himself completely. But (as scarcely needs saying) the confessional impulse, one motive for which this utterance of his expresses, was strong in Boswell. It is one aspect of his attachment to Johnson, as the episode of their probable quarrel over Boswell's frankness about his sexual irregularities suggests. Indeed, it was a feature of their friendship from the very beginning; of their fourth meeting he writes: "I then told my history to Mr. Johnson, which he listened to with attention." [51] The scene was to be repeated frequently, and not only with Johnson. Boswell left with Rousseau, "a 'Sketch of My Life,' in which I gave him the important incidents of my history and my melancholy apprehensions, and begged his advice and friendship." [52] In short, Boswell's famous fondness for cultivating great men was, in part at least, an expression of a longing to find a worthy (and sympathetic) confessor. Failing such a one, the Journals had to serve. In them, as his wife put it, he "embowelled" himself—"a good strong figure," Boswell remarks, and purgation with a vengeance.[53]

When he could not "extract" the melancholy by "writing down," he could sometimes stave it off by posting his Journal. As Johnson told him, occupation is what the mind requires in melancholy moments. Boswell did not always need the courses in chemistry or rope dancing that Johnson once recommended (nor even the "course of concubinage" that then suggested itself to him).[54] "This afternoon I had a return of my gloom," he writes on one occasion. "I walked out and was very uneasy. I returned to my inn, journalised, and recovered." [55] It is not merely labor that works the recovery, one suspects, but communion with the self, a communion reminding him, all absent-heartedness and dryness of the soul to the contrary, that that self still exists, if only because it can contemplate and record its own misery.

Boswell "will go through almost anything with a degree of satisfaction if I am to put an account of it in writing." [56] He makes the corollary of this proposition just as explicit. "I should live no more than I can record," he says, "as one should not have more corn growing than one can get in." [57] I suggest the essential equivalence in Boswell's mind of his life and his account of it. As the simile implies, Boswell's journalizing is the exercise of a kind of psychic economy. Recollection, he frequently remarks, is a treasure. Boswell was greedy for experience; his every reader recognizes as much. And he was also miserly with it. The existence of volume after volume of these records of himself expresses an almost desperate unwillingness to permit the least fraction of the past—even the painful or trivial past—to disappear beyond recall and suggests that, for him, such disappearances, if permitted to occur, constituted a diminution of himself, a kind of death. An unrecorded day passes quickly into oblivion, and Boswell was much afraid of oblivion. To be sure, he sometimes sought it in drink. But, when he achieved it, he did so, in a sense, against his will: "I was sadly intoxicated. *Perdidi diem.*" [58]

Boswell hopes, of course, that his Journals will survive him, that in them he will be "embalmed." [59] When he sees how other men's journals are "treated as lumber," he cannot but "moralize" on what may become of his own. But their usefulness to him, not their future fate, is at last the test, for "nothing is equally important to a man with himself." [60] Boswell's Journals are an attempt to preserve that self in being by laying up the treasure of the past, those evanescent moments of consciousness that, as we have seen, constitute life for him. The trouble with identifying reality with the passing moment is that the moment passes. Boswell's journalizing is, in one of its aspects, the attempt to arrest that process, to substitute something like permanence for that restless change. The Journals do not record only those moments that he obviously cherishes but, as nearly as possible, *all* moments. They thereby express Boswell's love of life; but they do so indirectly, negatively, as a function of his fear of oblivion—that death to which the consciousness of anything, even pain, is preferable. Boswell requires proofs of his own existence, and these the Journals and the act of journalizing provide. Without them, he feels unreal to himself.

Basically, Boswell wishes to be always all of Boswell, the sum of his moments of consciousness, whatever that may be. He is never certain of his own nature for long. Insecure in the tenure of his identity, Boswell, especially in his early years, seeks in the world about him figures from whom he can draw, not only strength (though that is important to him), but other qualities that will enlarge and somehow define him. "Be vigorous. Be Temple," he adjures himself; "Be pious like Pitfour." [61] "I was quite happy, quite Digges," he congratulates himself on one occasion.[62] The point is that he *knows* Temple and Pitfour and Digges; if he can "be" them (or at least detect in himself points of comparison with them), then he can know what *he* is. He has many such models, and they are remarkably various. Johnson is one. But so are Sir Richard Steele and Shakespeare, Walton, Donne, Addison, and Demosthenes. Nor does he confine himself to actual persons.

Over and over again, Boswell casts himself in roles of his or others' invention. Now he is Macheath, now vaguely the hero of a novel, now a "morose don," Millamant, a Man of Pleasure, Rousseau's ambassador to Corsica, an amorous Spaniard, a castaway, an officer on a German campaign, Prince Hal.

Some of these fancies persist longer or recur more frequently than others. But the very length of the list suggests his sense of the insufficiency of his own unfixed character. He is really nothing or at best "Jamie Boswell, without any respect." To be sure, this particular sort of instability declines in importance fairly soon. On August 9, 1764, at Brunswick, he at last becomes capable of writing:

> I saw my error in suffering so much from the contemplation of others. I can never be them, therefore let me not vainly attempt it in imagination. . . . I must be Mr. Boswell of Auchinleck, and no other. Let me make him as perfect as possible. . . . I recollected my moments of despair when I did not value myself at sixpence, because, forsooth, I was but an individual, and an individual is nothing in the multitude of beings. Whereas *I* am all to myself. I have but one existence. If it is a mad one, I cannot help it. I must do my best.[63]

In the very next paragraph he seeks in imagination assurances of the friendship of Johnson, "so that I might march under his protection while he lived, and after his death, imagine that his shade beckoned me to the skies."[64] But never after this was he so desperately a man in search of a character.

His impulse to identify himself with others persists however. He seeks to enlarge himself by experiencing the world as he imagines others to experience it. Thus in 1772 he enjoys a meeting with his fellow proprietors of *The London Magazine*, an evening

> quite in the style of London editors. . . . I was a man of considerable consequence. The place of our meeting, St. Paul's Church-

> yard, the sound of St. Paul's clock striking the hours, the busy and bustling countenances of the partners around me, all contributed to give me a complete sensation of the kind. I hugged myself in it. I thought how different this was from the usual objects of a Scots laird.[65]

Boswell does not for a moment believe that he was *really* "a man of considerable consequence." Circumstances having allowed him to assume that role for an evening, he simply thinks himself into the skin of such a person, acquiring thereby some permanent sense of what the world feels like to that kind of man.

But the persons with whom Boswell identified himself and whose sensations and emotions he attempted to feel were not always so respectable as a London editor. Sometimes the dark side of his nature is revealed in his choice of an object for this sort of interest—condemned men, for instance. "I always use to compare the conduct of malefactors with what I suppose my conduct might be," he says in explanation of the fascination executions always held for him.[66] One effect of such passages is to suggest that Boswell is indeed preparing for the moment when his disguises fall away and he is found out and led off to be punished. He cannot put it thus plainly to himself; but the hint is there. In any event, his interest in criminals was marked, even excessive, at least from the point of view of its effect on his worldly prospects. Boswell's sympathy with his poorer clients was sometimes so extreme as to get him into trouble with his seniors. His desperate efforts on behalf of John Reid, a sheep-stealer whom he defended, almost involved him in a duel with the son of a judge whose impartiality he had impugned.

Without denying Boswell the great credit due him for these largely selfless labors, we may legitimately suppose his efforts in this line to suggest something besides his undoubted generosity of spirit. The criminal personality had, from the start, both repelled and attracted him. On the one hand, there is his fear of highwaymen, a fear that he feels almost every time he sets out on a journey. On the other hand, there is his fascination with Captain Macheath, the highwayman hero of *The Beggar's Opera.* This seems to have been his favorite theatrical piece. Even the harassments that attended the last years of his life did not prevent him from seeing it when the opportunity offered.[67] And Macheath, as Pottle points out,[68] dominates the entire *London Journal.* A prisoner whom Boswell visits on the eve of execution he describes as "just a Macheath. He was dressed in a white coat and blue silk vest and silver, with his hair neatly queued and a silver-laced hat, smartly cocked." [69] The execution the next day of this dashing figure so depresses Boswell that he cannot sleep alone and must share a bed with his friend Erskine. But Macheath was to rise again, in the person of Boswell who, for an evening, styles himself "Macdonald" and accompanies two prostitutes to a tavern.

> "Waiter," said I, "I have got here a couple of human beings; I don't know how they'll do." "I'll look, your Honour," cried he, and with inimitable effrontery stared them in the face and then cried, "They'll do very well." "What," said I, "are they good fellow-creatures? Bring them up, then." We were shown into a good room and had a bottle of sherry before us in a minute. I surveyed my seraglio and found them both good subjects for amorous play. I toyed with them and drank about and sung *Youth's the Season* and thought myself Captain Macheath; and then I solaced my existence with them, one after the other, according to their seniority.[70]

Boswell clearly has in mind Act II, scene i, of *The Beggar's Opera,* where Macheath, newly escaped from Newgate but about to be recaptured, summons Jenny Diver and the rest to an inn to entertain him. And Boswell's awareness of himself as an actor in a scene is quite as much a pleasure to him as is the "solace" he takes.

Sometimes his parts are not so glamorous, so literary. In 1763, the year of the incident just recounted, on the night of the king's birthday,

> I dressed myself in my second-mourning suit, in which I had been powdered many months, dirty buckskin breeches, and black stockings, a shirt of Lord Eglinton's which I had worn two days, and little round hat with tarnished silver lace belonging to a disbanded officer of the Royal Volunteers. I had in my hand an old oaken stick battered against the pavement. And was I not a complete blackguard I went to the Park, picked up a low brimstone, called myself a barber, and agreed with her for sixpence. . . . I then . . . came to Ashley's Punch-house and drank three threepenny bowls. In the Strand I picked up a little profligate wretch and gave her sixpence. She allowed me entrance. But the miscreant refused me performance. . . . "Brother soldiers," said I, "should not a half-pay officer r-g-r for sixpence? And here has she used me so and so." I got them on my side, and I abused her in blackguard style, and then left them. At Whitehall I picked up another girl to whom I called myself a highwayman and told her I had no money and begged she would trust me. But she would not. My vanity was somewhat gratified tonight that, notwithstanding of my dress, I was always taken for a gentleman in disguise.[71]

Here the highwayman is no elegant Macheath, but brother to a barber and an outrageous half-pay officer. And here is Boswell's enlargement of himself at its darkest. A critic has called this episode "an archetypal descent to the underworld" [72]—an assertion that claims too much for even Boswell's talent for staging experience. Is that oaken stick his golden bough? The true parallel seems to me at once vaguer and more interesting. Boswell is not echoing anything; he is anticipating something. He is a kind of comic Faust, a bourgeois hero of experience.

Boswell's identification of himself with others, his assumption of roles, expresses his desire to heighten the ordinary pleasures of life by experiencing them doubly, in two persons. And it also expresses an appetite for classes of experience foreign to his usual, conscious, daylight self—brutality, degradation, even death. He is pleased, of course, that he does not entirely pass out of himself into the characters he assumes ("I was always taken for a gentleman in disguise"); but still there is that desire to escape from himself into darkness at the same time that he is enlarging himself by arranging to encounter the world through another man's senses. The contradiction between these impulses—toward the extension and toward the abandonment of his personality—is merely apparent, for both issue from Boswell's anxious dissatisfaction with his self as it ordinarily appears to him.

In the narration of the events of his "blackguard" night, Boswell strikes another note that, in combination with its occurrences elsewhere, reveals something interesting about him. Having told one of the girls that he had no money, he "begged that she would trust" him. During his evening as Macdonald, he had made a similar proposition to a Miss Watts and to his girls at the tavern, and they had been willing to oblige, their compliance adding to his pleasure. His motive was not, it seems clear, simple economy. Pathetic as it may seem, Boswell is seeking among these women assurances of his own personal worth. Boswell often doubted that worth, especially as it appeared in the eyes of women.

It has been remarked that, though Boswell irresistibly gravitated toward great men, he did not feel the same attraction toward remarkable women. Belle de Zuylen[73] is an exception, of course; but one fact that emerges from his account of his affair with her is that he could never feel easy in her presence. It seems to be a fact that only among prostitutes or, at best, among such notorious women as Mary Caroline Rudd[74] could he enjoy that "consciousness that he is the superior person" that he once declared to be essential.[75] Perhaps the root of the matter was his fear (occasionally confirmed[76]) of impotence; he could not be entirely at ease with Louisa "until my ability was known."[77] Hence, perhaps, his rather unattractive pride in good performance. In normal health, he seems to have been capable enough. Indeed, on occasion he reputedly performed prodigies. Now and then—as in his affair with Rousseau's mistress—one suspects that he was spurred on as much by the wish to demonstrate something as by simple desire. Perhaps part of his energy derived from his emulation of Rousseau, his wish to be that great man. And certain asterisks that appear from time to time in his Journals seem to denote, not only the nights in which he made love to his wife, but also the number of times he did so. It may be, in short, that Boswell is that Freudian cliché, the Don Juan whose sexual athleticism disguises strong doubts about his manliness.

In any case, Boswell's relations with women were a trouble to him and forced him, as we have seen, to the pitiable extreme of seeking from whores the strongest proof that they could supply, the sacrifice of their fee, that he is the engaging fellow he likes to think himself. So characteristic of him is this test of his worthiness that he tries it on the woman he is to marry. "Will you, then, knowing me fully, accept of me for your husband as I now am;—not the heir of Auchinleck, but one who has had his time of the world, and is henceforth to expect no more than £100 a year?" he asks her.[78] "This was truly romantic," he confides to his Journal, "and perhaps too severe a trial of a woman of so much good sense and so high a character."[79] The implication is that it would not be too severe a trial of other sorts of woman—a fact affirming the connection suggested here. And the trial—Boswell's words in this entry to the contrary—is not only of her, but of him. Boswell is contriving to discover, not whether she is a worthy enough person to take him as he is, but whether he is, in his own person, worthy enough to be chosen. Her qualities, as the story of their courtship makes clear, are not in question; his are. Her answer gladdens him. It "did me more real honour than anything I have met with in my life," he writes.[80] Her response is, in short, proof that he deserves her.

Boswell, then, betrays in his Journals a radical uncertainty about his own nature and his own worth. Thus, uncertainty is connected—partly as a cause and partly as a consequence—with Boswell's difficult relations with his father and with his notions of family.

It is a commonplace of opinion about Boswell that his passion for great men (Dr. Johnson, of course, in particular) expresses his desire to substitute an understanding, though still authoritative, figure for the cold and rigid master of Auchinleck—a fatherly man for someone who is simply a father. Boswell's scheme to enter the Guards, his prolonged Grand Tour, his almost annual jaunts to London, his wish for an English practice, his ambitions as an author are all capable of interpretation as efforts to escape his father's restrictively conventional will. Insofar as it is true that a happy and fulfilled Boswell would never have written the Journals, we owe his father a great debt. The trouble was that Boswell could not reject out of hand the chilly virtues that his father represented, for they were virtues he admired, though he could not attain them. "I was healthy and cheerful, and just Father," he says on one occasion,* associating what he desires to be, but so often is not, with his parent's character. He can ask why there should not be "a diversity of characters in the succession of lairds," but he always suspects that his difference from his father is a crippling deficiency.[81] In short, the sanctions of his father's ideal of character and conduct appeared so strong to Boswell that he was as incapable of effectively rebelling against it as he was of living up to it. In this paralyzing situation Boswell passed his entire life, and it is the greatest possible compliment to him that he managed to achieve anything at all, either along the lines his father laid down or along those that his sense of his own private powers suggested.

* *Germany and Switzerland*, p. 99. One does not easily associate cheer, in any ordinary sense of the term, with the senior Boswell. All it means here, I think, is "not melancholy." For much of his life, cheer could mean no more to Boswell.

Again and again he resolved to be the man that his father desired him to be. This is the meaning, for instance, of the commands that at one period in his life he constantly laid on himself.

> You *must* do well and be a good, worthy, respected man. . . . Learn *retenue*. Pray do. . . . Be one day without talking of self or repeating. . . . Be steady. . . . *Be retenu*. . . . Go to bed exact at twelve. . . . *Think*. Be firm. . . . *Plan*. . . . Think. Maintain character gained at Utrecht, nor ever rave. Mem. Father.*

And it is part of the meaning of the tears that he shed at "the pathetic scene between the old King and his son" in *Henry IV, Part II*. He seems to have in mind the scene in Act IV, scene v, where the father reproaches the son for wishing him dead and predicts that evil days will follow.

> Harry the Fifth is crowned! Up, Vanity!
> Down, royal state! all you sage counsellors, hence!
> And to the English court assemble now,
> From every region, apes of idleness!
> Now, neighbour confines, purge you of your scum:
> Have you a ruffian that will swear, drink, dance,
> Revel the night, rob, murder, and commit
> The oldest sins the newest kind of ways?
> Be happy, he will trouble you no more
>
> . . .
>
> England shall give him office, honour, might;
> For the fifth Harry from curb'd license plucks
> The muzzle of restraint. . . .

Prince Hal denies the accusation and speaks of his reformation:

> if I do feign,
> O! let me in my present wildness die

* *Holland*, pp. 24, 47, 86, 88, 95. These lines are from his memorandums, which are often in the imperative mode; a director, a moral overseer, was always with him.

And never live to show the incredulous world
The noble change that I have purposed.[83]

Like Mill, who wept at a passage in Marmontel's memoirs describing the death of a father and the new independence and authority of a son, Boswell is moved by the enactment of matters close to his heart on which it is painful for him to reflect. His desire for a dignified discussion and reconciliation of the differences between him and his father is dramatized; the unlikelihood of such a meeting is one source of his distress. And his no-doubt-complicated feelings about the prospect of his father's death, no matter how distant in time that event may be, are probably trying to force their way into consciousness. Thoughts of his father's death are ordinarily matter for dreams, dreams that evoke recollections of the "natural affection and tenderness of my young years." [84] It is tempting to say that Boswell's dreams and his response to the play express a disguised desire for his father's death. Perhaps. On the other hand, this much is certain: consciously, at least, Boswell always loved his father. Interestingly and pathetically, it was an affection that had in it "much of the tenderness of a child"; that is to say, it is associated in his mind with the time when he did not have to *deserve* his father's esteem.

Unlike Prince Hal, of course, Boswell never achieved the "noble change" that he "purposed"; he never revived for long his father's early affection for him. And, accepting as he did, in at least one part of his mind, his father's notions of the character proper to an heir of Auchinleck, he was forced to doubt the sufficiency and independent value of his own very different personality. Now and again, he could be content with his odd self. "I am in reality an original character," writes Boswell in Berlin. "Let me moderate and cultivate my originality. . . . Let me then be Boswell and render him as fine a fellow as possible." [85] But such occasions are relatively rare and are most likely to occur when, as here, he is far from home. In Edinburgh and at Auchinleck the "original" in Boswell he often regards with almost as much apprehensiveness and mistrust as does his father.

Against his own and his father's dissatisfaction with him, however, Bowell had one interesting defense. This was his sense of family, which was perhaps extravagant even in an age when family meant much more than it does today. Normally, a man of good family like Boswell had to conceive of himself in at least two ways: first, as a particular individual with his own talents and passions and, second, as an heir, the representative of his family in a particular generation, the link binding the future to the past. For men like Boswell's father, there was little conflict between these two roles. But for Boswell himself the conflict was large and painful. One way of expressing those difficulties with his father that we have just been examining is to say that they consist in the father's constantly reminding the son of this conflict and the son's constant struggle to end it. So much Boswell's response to that scene in *Henry IV, Part II,* makes clear; the play has to do with kings and princes, the family at its most dynastic. On the face of it, one would expect Boswell to minimize the reality of the split. One way of doing this would be to deny, if only to himself, the importance of the second of his roles, the familial one. But Boswell does precisely the opposite. He takes what must have seemed to his father the strange position of going the old man one better in his loyalty to the family and name of Boswell.

Boswell states his notions of family in connection with two great subjects—his father's remarriage and the entail that Boswell proposes, which would confine the inheritance of Auchinleck to male heirs. In the first of these, Boswell had some worldly interest. It was possible, he seems to have thought, that his stepmother might further alienate him from his father's already weak affections; and he knew that, if she bore his father children, their share in the inheritance would, at very least, diminish what he and his brothers would receive.[86] But, in the case of the proposed entail, Boswell's motives were, to say the least, disinterested. As his wife frequently and vigorously reminded him, its effect would be to disinherit his own children, for at the time he had only daughters.

At last, to be sure, Boswell compromised, and the estate was entailed on male heirs descended from his great-grandfather, an arrangement that satisfied him while it excluded one David Boswell, a dancing master to whom his father violently objected and whose heirs might have succeeded to the title had Boswell's original plan been adopted.[87] But he did not reach this point for a long time.

It is difficult to understand exactly what the grounds of Boswell's "feudal principles" were. On the one hand, they seem rather literary, an impractical carrying over into everyday life of those sentiments that made the English of that period so receptive to Gothic novels, the poems of Ossian, and Percy's *Reliques*. "The Old Castle, the romantic rocks and woods of Auchinleck, must never be forsaken" [88] says Boswell, in tones that recall American Southerners vainly trying to perpetuate an unreal past. Thus, he requests one of his brothers to sign an oath, in the presence of two clergymen for chaplains and some gardeners (most of them children) to represent a loyal tenantry, in which the brother promises to give "reasonable obedience" to the representative of the "ancient family of Auchinleck." This oath, given in the ruins of the old house, is declared to be "according to the usage of the family," as though it were a tradition hallowed by time instead of the Boswellian invention it is.[89]

The feelings attendant on such carryings-on, however foolish they appear, were an important part of Boswell's life, and he sought out occasions for experiencing them. It was partly in quest of such sensation, for instance, that he toured the Hebrides with Johnson. He delights in importing the past into the present.

> To see Mr. Samuel Johnson lying in Prince Charles's bed, in the Isle of Skye, in the house of Miss Flora Macdonald, struck me with such a group of ideas as it is not easy for words to describe as the mind perceives them.[90]

And at Iona he takes pleasure in the "antiquity and remoteness of the place." He exults "in thinking that the solemn scenes of piety ever remain the same," no matter what the effects of "the cares and follies of life" may be. In the cathedral there, he reads aloud a sermon and feels "a serious joy in hearing my voice, while it was filled with Ogden's admirable eloquence, resounding in the ancient cathedral of Icolmkill." [91] Boswell here is enjoying the confrontation of his mortality with the permanence of these relics of the past. His emotions, one senses, are gently melancholy, but comfortable; permanence, of whatever sort, is something that Boswell cherishes, and Iona and Auchinleck embody it.

I have spoken of Boswell's desire to enlarge himself by encountering the world as he imagines others encounter it. His "feudal principles" serve him in rather the same way. In expressing them, he experiences feelings that he holds to be proper to persons as remote from him in time as Corsica, say, was remote in space or Macheath in character. Moreover, he seeks to dignify his life by associating himself with things fixed and lasting. In short, his love of family and interest in heritable things is another of his stays against confusion. And there is more to it than this. Boswell's passion for family is, I have said, his way of living up to his responsibilities as heir of Auchinleck. But it is a partial way, emphasizing only that portion of his duties that he knew himself fully capable of performing. As his difficulties with his father declare, Boswell could not maintain the public posture of a dour man of affairs that his role required. But that, after all, is not the sum of an heir's duties. He has also his merely biological function, as the link joining past to future. He could perform this function, or, if he could not, he could make sure that the effect was the same, that someone of his name inherited the estate.

This may well be the principal meaning of his insistence on male inheritance and male inheritance only—that thereby the identity of the family would be preserved. For him, "the real family" consists of the sons, and them alone.[92]

> It will not do to say a grandson by a daughter is as near as a grandson by a son. It leads into a nice disquisition in natural philosophy. I say the *stamen* is derived from the *man*. The woman is only like the ground where a tree is planted. A grandson by a daughter has no connection with my original stock. A new race is begun by a father of another name.*

Perhaps Boswell has been reading Aeschylus' *Eumenides*, where a similar biological theory is put forward. In any case, the name, the identity of his family, is what he is bent on preserving. "The idea of the Old Castle of Auchinleck going to a female in exclusion of *Boswells* was horrid," he writes.[93] It is significant that his objections to his father's plan abate soon after the birth of his son Alexander on October 9, 1775; Boswell has performed his duty or that portion of it that he can perform. Now he can descend to good sense and consider once more the claims of his private self. "I thought for a little that a man should place his pride and his happiness in his own individuality, and endeavour to be as rich and as renowned and as happy as he can," Boswell writes on the last day of that year. "I considered that Dr. Johnson is as well as if he belonged to a *family*." [94]

* *Wife*, p. 255. The passage is almost hysterical. Boswell continues: "Let females be well portioned. Let them enjoy liberally what is naturally intended for them. . . . But for goodness' sake, let us not make feudal lords, let us not make barons of them. As well might we equip them with breeches, swords, and gold-laced hats." Altogether the passage seems to express not so much a rational loyalty to the principle of male inheritance as it does a kind of panic at the thought of feminine power.

Boswell's editors speak of the "unreasonable and tedious hold" that his "feudal" ideas had on him.[95] Tedious his enunciations of them may be, but, rightly understood, the ideas themselves are not at all unreasonable. Boswell felt his family responsibilities as strongly as any father could wish; but, knowing something of himself, he recognized that he could not support them all. What he could do, he did; one way or another, by process of law or by fathering a son, he was determined to perform his family duty to the past and the future, and in this he succeeded. This determination, I suggest, was a virtue of the defects of his character. His willingness to sink himself into the role of the transmitter of a name, indeed his very emphasis on the name Boswell, expresses the low estimate which he shared with his father of himself as a particular bearer of it. As *James* Boswell he is a failure, but as James *Boswell* he may be a success.

Boswell, I have been suggesting in these pages, was a man unwilling to come to rest in himself, an unwillingness that expresses his uncertainty of the worth of that self. In our jargon, he was anxious, insecure. In large part, I think, the attraction that he exercises for many modern readers issues from a sense of shared weakness. Surely it is one of Boswell's greatest achievements that he managed to set down how it feels to live in that uncomfortable relationship with oneself. But this sympathetic response of ours to Boswell is incomplete. For the Journals are not, finally, a chronicle of weakness.

To understand what is strong in them we must first name and understand one other thing that he had in common with his serious modern readers: an urban consciousness, which I take to be characteristic of most twentieth-century intellectual life. To such a consciousness, the city is not only the locus of power, wealth, and worldly opportunity, but a condition of life so stimulating to the spirit that the moral exhaustion that such stimulation often entails seems a fair price to pay. Boswell paid that price, we know. The desperate melancholy that he suffered in Holland, for instance, expressed the psychic depletion in which his year in London had quite naturally resulted. Even in Edinburgh, he could experience that terror of the city which, though it is not peculiar to the sort of person with whom we are concerned here, is peculiarly painful to him, for it is caused by something he loves:

> I felt that my nerves were yet weak at times, for I had a sensation of being wild and timorous, as if I had been for years in the country, and all the objects in the town—the houses, the coaches, the people—hurt me in an unaccountable manner.[96]

Still, the stimulation was worth it. Loyal as he was to the idea of Auchinleck, Boswell did not really wish to live there. He preferred Edinburgh to the country and London to either. The city is the home of possibility. "I wanted to be something," Boswell writes in explanation of his youthful discontent with Scotland, and to be something he came to London. There, he could be any number of things.

The great question was, Could he be Boswell? Or, rather, Was there a Boswell to be? The answer, as I said earlier, was, Not yet. It was a time for trying on roles, disguises even; London was a theater in which Boswell might play what parts he chose (Boswell himself seems nearly conscious of the aptness of this metaphor in his identification of himself with West Digges, an actor, and Macheath).* And he continues this project all his life. As late as 1790, he imitates a watchman by calling an early-morning hour in the streets[97]—a trivial example, perhaps, but expressive of his persistence in using the anonymity that the city confers.

* As Jeffrey Hart remarks in "Some Thoughts on Johnson as Hero," *Johnsonian Studies* (Cairo, 1962), p. 24, Boswell is among the first, in literature or out of it, to explore "those transformations of self which the peculiar conditions of the modern city make possible."

What I mean to suggest here is that Boswell's adoption of roles and disguises, of which I earlier made much as evidence of his uncertainty about his own nature and the weakness of his sense of his own identity, has a positive function, too. Boswell desires among other things to *enlarge* himself, to incorporate within himself as many kinds of experience as possible; and this is owing, not only to his fears about himself, but also to his confidence that he has in him something that demands this special diet. "Sir," said Garrick to him in 1763, "you will be a very great man." [98] It is difficult to know how seriously Garrick meant this. But Johnson, too, had, from the first, a good opinion of him; and Rousseau acknowledged that Boswell's claims to distinction were not groundless. "I think there is a bloom about me of something more distinguished than the generality of mankind," Boswell writes, reflecting on Garrick's prediction.[99] This bloom required nourishment if it were to swell into fruit. And such nourishment, I maintain, the roles Boswell played provided. So did his watchful self-awareness, always eager to register the variations in his consciousness. Boswell experiences; he experiences himself experiencing; in his Journals he re-experiences, so to speak, his self in each of these postures. By an act of will, he summons himself as fully as possible into his own consciousness.

Which is to say that he creates himself. It is chiefly this that I had in mind when I spoke of Boswell's energies as having an aesthetic end in view. Boswell manipulates experience, simulates, contrives, to the purpose of shaping a life. Life, we have seen, he implicitly conceives as inescapably the sum of moments of consciousness. To a degree, he is helpless, passive before the flux of sensation that his intercourse with the world provides. But, to almost as great a degree, he is active. He exercises his will in order to seek out certain materials of consciousness that will make the final product as interesting, various, and comprehensive as possible. Coherence and comeliness of his creation he unfortunately could not achieve, though he struggled to do so. His life, as it is recorded in his Journals but primarily as it was present to his consciousness, is nevertheless a work of willed, deliberate, if defective, art. The oddness of Boswell's transactions with reality issues from weaknesses that we may conveniently term neurotic. But it is as true of Boswell as it is of others whose accounts of their lives are examined in this study that weakness is intimately bound up with strength. It is what strength practices on, the necessary, ambiguous angel with which a man wrestles through the night for the reward, like Jacob's, of an identity, a name.

V

CONCLUSION

Agents of the New

All that is required of the autobiographer—it is a very large "all"—is that his language and his design answer to the truth of his experience. We cannot ascertain whether it in fact does, for obviously we can have no independent check on how it felt to live his life. But he must convince us that his book is living up to the truth. When he succeeds, it does not much matter that here and there we may correct a detail in his account, and this is one reason why, as I warned the reader at the outset, I here concern myself so little with the errors and suppressions of these writers. In achieving this success, what counts is the autobiographer's manner—his way with language, and his sense of form. His manner has to do not only with how he tells his truth; it is itself that truth.

Thus it is, for instance, that Gibbon's sentences declare him to be—in contrast with Fox, say—a man of literary consciousness. Their formality, their deliberate structure, their aspect as controlled things announce his essential solidarity with the dominant culture and the men in confident possession of it. But certain mannerisms of his style speak to what is perhaps the individuality of his notions about himself. The famous balance of those sentences reinforces, if it does not by itself define, his sense of the precariousness of human happiness. His fondness for the periodic sentence, in which the exact weight and relationship of the parts are to be understood only at last, expresses his concern, as historian of himself, with eventuality, with the result in the light of which all antecedent occasions declare their true importance.

And so it is with all the autobiographers discussed here. The vigor, particularity, and eccentricity of Roger North's vocabulary and sentence structure—in these matters he most resembles John Aubrey, that other treasurer of oddity and the past—give us our sense of him as one in love with the surfaces of things and constantly in touch with them. John Bunyan's prose is, as we have seen, full of plain names for plain things and of verbs and nouns that endow psychic and spiritual intangibles with vivid actuality, accomplishing thereby much of the main business of his book. George Fox's *Journal,* too, has this virtue. But it is flawed, and the flaw, like the strength of the book, is in the style. The syntax is often monotonous, and the monotony is traceable to Fox's dependence on mere sequence as a narrative principle. This weakness, I have said, characterizes many of the lesser Quaker autobiographies; that is to say, stylistic weakness is what makes them lesser. The virtues that these books display appear when the authors concentrate on a particular event. Thus, John Woolman is at his best when he is being urgently meticulous in describing a vision, his particularity being, like Bunyan's and Fox's, in the service of credibility. So, too, with Haime and Told, and Haime especially has some of Bunyan's other strengths. In William Cowper, however, we come on something new. His record, like those of his best predecessors, is close and honest in its account of events. But it is something else as well; it is literary. As his allusions and metaphors demonstrate, his education had provided him a fluent and flexible vocabulary of feeling. Increasingly from his time onward, autobiographers were to be men similarly equipped to find access to themselves.

Boswell is, as usual, a special case. In a sense, he has no style, though almost any of his paragraphs is instantly identifiable to the experienced ear. But his distinctive quality is not, first of all, a matter of language. Now and then, as when he speaks of hugging himself with self-satisfaction, he hits on the perfect word. Ordinarily his stylistic virtues are negative; his words do not obtrude. Physical objects, men, ideas exist in his response to them, a response that his language conveys without drawing much attention to itself. A more fruitful way of coming to grips with the peculiar tone of the Journals is to think of how it feels to read them. We read a man, not a book. What happens, happens *now*. Boswell does not simply retail what Johnson told him. Both are present at this instant on the page. The distinctive effect of all but the dullest entries is a special kind of intensity; we are unremittingly aware of each day as the point of Boswell's furthest penetration into the future. Such intensity any diarist might theoretically achieve, as the autobiographer, looking back over a stretch of time, almost necessarily cannot. (Indeed, the dailiness of a diary, the source of its possible strength, may be a flaw in an autobiography; witness Fox's, which is almost as much a book of moments as Boswell's, but by accident.) But the intensity of Boswell's account has to do with our sense that he has, at the moment of writing, no more assurance than we have in our own lives of what the morrow will bring. The terrors of the past may be painful for an autobiographer to recall; but at least they are known, at least they have been survived. In reading Boswell, we live always at the leading edge of experience.

Still, it is Boswell's experience. For us, it is art, though art that takes part of its effect from our direct sense of our own precarious tenure of happiness and life itself. But this effect alone does not entirely account for the pleasure that Boswell gives us. Only for Boswell himself was that aspect of his Journals the first reality. "The truth is, that the spectators are always in their senses," said Dr. Johnson, contradicting the notion that the illusion produced by a drama must or may be absolute.[1] Nor do we forget ourselves entirely as we read ourselves into Boswell's skin. In the Journals, as W. H. Auden remarked in a review quoted earlier, we confront ourselves; but, mercifully, through the medium of art. "Objects which in themselves we view with pain," says Aristotle in the *Poetics*, "we delight to contemplate when reproduced with minute fidelity: such as the forms of the most ignoble animals and of dead bodies" [2]—and of our own natures. That profound mystery of art of which Aristotle speaks lies near the source of our pleasure in all autobiographical writing. But it has a special relationship to Boswell's work. I said earlier that Boswell's energies had a partly aesthetic end in view. Here is one explanation of that end. For Boswell, too, his Journals became, in the lapse of time, a work of art. Reading in them, he could "delight to contemplate" himself, a pleasure not otherwise always open to him.

So far, we have been speaking of the autobiographer's manner chiefly as having to do with his language. But form, its other aspect, is perhaps even more important. Particular chapters have spoken of the success of these men in finding a form answerable to their experience. Perhaps "finding," implying intention as it does, is not quite the word, or not always. But, for better or worse, the formal aspect of these books means something in every case. The diffusion of Roger North's account of himself among the *Lives* of his brothers and the relative indifference to himself implied by the aimless organization and perfunctoriness of *Notes of Mee* are what gives us our knowledge that he was a man willing to spend himself among others and generously eager to do so among his brothers. Gibbon's control is so sure that, as one critic has put it: "For the first time we have an autobiography which reviews a whole life as the shaping and fruition of a specific skill devoted to one absorbing enterprise." [3] His book is the history of a historian, and nothing that did not contribute to that aspect of him is admitted. I have said that Gibbon acknowledges that a good deal more than one might expect had a share in what he became, and it is partly this acknowledgment that gives his book its somber interest. But to write of oneself only as a historian is to take oneself very calmly indeed. The formal principle that he adopted no doubt accounts, in large part, for the impression Gibbon leaves of speaking as though he were himself a Roman Empire.

This calmness of Gibbon's has a moral aspect, which is what I meant when I said earlier that he manages to contain his experience. Gibbon is at pains to declare that he has not made his fate; but neither has his fate made him. Refusing to be mastered by life at the same time that he acknowledges that he has not himself mastered it, Gibbon quietly lays claim to the virtues of strength and honesty. Our sense of these virtues in him is owing at least partly to the rigorous form of his book. His aesthetic intention cannot have been easy to achieve. (Indeed, in his own person he did not achieve it, for it was not Gibbon who set the manuscript in order; but the made thing was there, ready to be found, when he died.) Nor can the moral life that it records have been easy to live. Still, there it is before us, a fact, a human possibility, and, in its own excellence, as exemplary as Bunyan's.

In its own excellence. But that excellence, my study has been suggesting, is not possible for most of us. Our most keenly felt realities are not thus to be ordered and subdued. For us, Boswell and Bunyan and Cowper are the exemplars—Boswell as the endurer and Bunyan and Cowper as the victors.

Our interest in Wordsworth and Mill is continuous with an interest in these earlier men. A sympathetic response to any of these autobiographies expresses, in part, a willingness to ratify these accounts as in some sense conformable to our own modes of experience. But we must assess the moral value of our psychic suffering at a lower value than we do theirs. In earlier chapters, I praised the heroism of those men of religion who survived excursions into insanity. But to the victories over themselves that they achieved the modern reader, should he think of aspiring to the dignity of these men, must have an ambiguous response. Part of what made their lives heroic was their loneliness. Even in the nineteenth century, the sufferer might feel, in Mill's words,

> that mine was not an interesting, or in any way respectable distress. There was nothing in it to attract sympathy. Advice, if I had known where to seek it, would have been most precious.[4]

It was partly to give such advice or at least to assure others that their sufferings were not unexampled that Bunyan and Cowper and the rest wrote their books. In this project, as collaborators with other forces in the culture, they have at last been successful. Neurotic suffering is nowadays a very "respectable distress"—perhaps too respectable. And hence it has lost for us, in our own experience of it, the heroic aspect it has in the accounts that those earlier men set down.

That may be a lucky thing. After the fact, the twice-born, even those of them whose second birth may be said to have occurred in the madhouse, have found in their sufferings a positive value—that cheerful and mournful wisdom of which Mill speaks.[5] The question remains, Is it worth it, either for the sufferer or for the culture that such "wisdom" has helped to shape? In regard to the man himself, the answer is reasonably plain. Whatever benefits he may have derived from an extreme experience of the sort that these autobiographies record, he would hesitate to recommend such suffering as an object of choice. At that price, even so magnificent an achievement as *Grace Abounding* or *The Pilgrim's Progress* is dearly bought; to be willing to pay it is to be sick already. Salvation, to be sure, might be recompense enough. At least some of these men received a sense of blessed intimacy with God as a return for their misery. But none of them deny that there are ways other than theirs to attain it. In short, to Bunyan and

Cowper and the others, these sufferings were at once hugely valuable and strenuously to be avoided.

It is impossible to speak so simply of the cultural consequences of the new attitudes toward private experience exemplified in these autobiographies. On the one hand, the benefits have obviously been enormous. To speak very broadly, one supposes that the great progress made during this century and the last toward more equitable social arrangements and institutions has been achieved partly as a result of the accession to the consciousness of literally millions of humble persons of a sense of their worth and dignity as individuals. A new way of thinking about themselves produced a new way of thinking about their world. Almost paradoxically, the high value that men came to put on private experiences, freeing them from impotent, accepting anonymity, encouraged them to combine with others to force the social recognition of their new conception of themselves on the public world. Self-consciousness is, that is to say, a subversive force.

Unhappily, it has proved capable of subverting good things as well as bad. Richard Hofstadter has recently associated the intellectual debasement of religious life in America with the Great Awakening of the eighteenth century, a movement in which one of the authors discussed in an earlier chapter, George Whitefield, played an important part and with which others considered here would have at least sympathized.[6] The confident and ignorant judgments of those who trust absolutely the intimations of their own minds have had in this country—and elsewhere, too, surely—unfortunate consequences, not only for religion, but for politics and the life of the mind. What one reviewer of Hofstadter's book called "a perfervid evangelicism divorced from intellectual discipline" [7] has much to answer for; and the autobiographers discussed here—or, if not they themselves, then their adherents and imitators—were its early voices.

Such effects, of course, these men neither intended nor foresaw. Thinking about their autobiographies, one is struck by how much and, at the same time, how little they understood the import of their experience. How much they understood the earlier chapters of this study have suggested. Bunyan's book encourages us, as contemplation of his life encouraged him, to believe that much of the darkness in a life is capable of explanation and control, though much is not. His trials impressed on him, as *Grace Abounding* impresses on us, the duty and possibility of health—relative health, at any rate. Cowper, too, struggled to make out the moral meaning of almost incomprehensible distress. For these men—and for the lesser figures discussed in these pages, though they are not always so explicit about it—extreme experience had seemed to suggest that the world had no meaning, or else a very ugly one. Sanity, when it returned, was grounded in right opinion about this matter.

These autobiographies are, every one of them, intended to testify to the goodness of God, a goodness that, having been called into ultimate question, their authors conceive to be therefore the more firmly established. They hold the experience of despair and recovery to have tested and confirmed the existence and beneficence of God. Just here, these writers reach the bounds of their comprehension—or, rather, exceed them. For increasingly the adventure in insanity, the voyage on which these religious men were among the first to embark, came to be valued for other reasons. I suggested earlier that it may not be a meaningless coincidence that, in the late eighteenth and early nineteenth centuries, the notion that Satan is the hero of *Paradise Lost* found its voice. By itself, this fact is slender evidence for my assertion. But surely it is no news to any reader of this book that the great interest of the nineteenth and twentieth centuries in the literature of darkness, imprisonment, alienation, torture, neurosis, perversion, and death suggests that we look to experience beyond the normal for newly valuable things. Whatever else those valuable things may be, they are not often evidence of the existence and beneficence of God. In short, history has conferred on many of the autobiographies considered here an accidental pathos. The kind of experience that their authors conceived to be at last a form of testimony to the truth of their faith has become the paradigm of a mode of consciousness that has done much to undermine it. From the faithful we have learned how to deny.

Hence the duality of our response to these men. With part of our minds, we can do nothing but admire them. To a degree, they all share the courage both to withstand and to understand that I remarked in Bunyan. They value the promptings of the unconscious, but not uncritically; they are open to new truth, but are not its prisoners. They suffer heroically and crown their heroism by surviving. The victory that their strength of self achieved we rightly praise, but for our uses it is compromised. They are exemplary men, but, if we should follow their example, we would not attain their relatively happy ends—at least not in their terms. For the consciousness of Christian salvation to which they came seems to many of us a piece of tremendous but now scarcely possible good luck.

However much of them we see in ourselves, however much we may owe them, we can never *be* them, even if we desired to. Of the versions of the self, the one most available to us is Boswell's. His kinship to Bunyan, Cowper, and the rest is plain, though Boswell's melancholy never for long found a focus, as theirs did in religion, and never came to so extreme a crisis, which, painful though it would have been, might have purged his distress. It is partly the inconclusiveness of his struggle that we share with him, for most of us are denied the dramatic resolution of our difficulties that may lead, on the one hand, to the kind of health that a Bunyan came to enjoy or, on the other hand, to deep and permanent insanity. Never delivered, never defeated, Boswell worked on at the very modern project of defining and creating himself. His dogged endurance lacks the drama of those ambiguous victories achieved by the men of religion. But it is not therefore less admirable. And its occasions or something like them are ours. Boswell is like many of us in being gauche, absurd, ambitious, feckless, and occasionally admirable. There is a modest heroism in daily confronting such facts about oneself with an ideal of wholeness and integrity of mind, a notion of steadiness and dignity; and heroism of that sort is still possible.

The benefits conferred on us by our accession to intense self-consciousness are, then, flawed. The redirection of attention to what goes on in the privacy of the self helped prepare the way for so liberating and therapeutic an art as psychoanalysis. But it also helped to create or at least to make current some of the very pains from which psychoanalysis helps to free us—affectlessness, greediness of conscience, despair. "Ask yourself whether you are happy, and you cease to be so," said Mill.[8] It was his "irrepressible self-consciousness" that asked the question and gave the melancholy answer. The wisdom that it has taught has been mournful as well as cheerful.

But, in any event, that wisdom has been our great concern since the late eighteenth century, when the self and its pain which had been invented and endured chiefly at the edges of society came to occupy—and preoccupy—those consciousnesses more nearly at the center of the culture.* Thus Wordsworth ex-

* John Newton, the evangelical clergyman and friend of Cowper, in the Preface intended for the first edition of Cowper's first volume of poems (1782) but not in fact included until the fifth edition, confidently anticipates the general recognition of the importance of purely inward experience. "At a time when . . . little is considered as deserving the name of knowledge, which will not stand the test of experiment, the very use of the term *experimental,* in religious concernments, is by too many unhappily rejected with disgust. But we well know, that they who affect to despise the inward feelings which religious persons speak of, and to treat them as enthusiasm and folly, have inward feelings of their own, which, though they would, they cannot suppress. . . . We must lose the remembrance of what we once

plicitly addresses himself in *The Prelude* to affirming that "the great thought by which we live" is revealed as a consequence of having undergone and survived the tortures of despair. For Carlyle, "the newest-attained progress in the Moral Development of man," his passage into "spiritual majority," consisted in experience like that recorded by the religious autobiographers. And Keats could ask: "Do you not see how necessary a World of Pains and troubles is to school an Intelligence and make it a Soul?" "Call the world if you Please 'The vale of Soul-making,'" he had just said; for souls do not truly exist "till they acquire identities, till each one is personally itself." [9]

The struggle of the soul to find and be itself is one of the great modern enterprises. Whether it will continue to be so is another question; whether it should, is another question still. Perhaps the answers have to do with how firmly we can share the confidence of these predecessors of ours in the utility and ultimate beneficence of pain.

---

were, before we can believe, that a man is satisfied with himself, merely because he endeavours to appear so. . . . We know that there are people, who, while by their looks and their language they wish to persuade us they are happy, would be glad to change their conditions with a dog. But in defiance of all their efforts, they continue to think, forebode, and tremble." *Poetical Works of William Cowper* (London, 1926) pp. 641–642.

NOTES

PART 1

1. *The Poetry of Experience: The Dramatic Monologue in Modern Literary Tradition,* (New York, 1963), pp. 11–12.

2. Alfred North Whitehead, *Science and the Modern World* (New York, 1948), pp. 52–55.

3. Jack Stillinger, ed., *The Early Draft of John Stuart Mill's "Autobiography"* (Urbana, Ill., 1961). And see Gertrude Himmelfarb's Introduction to Mill's *Essays on Politics and Culture* (Garden City, N.Y., 1963), pp. viii–x.

4. Goronwy Rees, *A Bundle of Sensations* (New York, 1961), pp. 15–16.

5. John Stuart Mill, *The Letters,* ed. Hugh S. R. Elliott (London, 1910), I, 42.

6. William James, *The Varieties of Religious Experience: A Study in Human Nature* (Rev. ed.; London and New York, 1902), p. 145.

7. *Ibid.*, p. 164.

8. *Boswell's Life,* II, 126.

9. Thomas Carlyle, *Sartor Resartus; On Heroes, Hero-Worship and the Heroic in History* (London and New York, 1908). The phrases are chapter titles in *Sartor Resartus.*

10. *Varieties of Religious Experience,* p. 135.

11. *Sartor Resartus,* pp. 125–126.

12. *Ibid.*, p. 128.

13. *Ibid.*, pp. 137–138.

14. Michael St. John Packe, *The Life of John Stuart Mill* (New York, 1954), p. 79.

15. John Stuart Mill, *On Bentham and Coleridge* (London, 1950), pp. 62–63.

16. *Ibid.*, p. 62.

17. Matthew Arnold, "Memorial Verses: April, 1850," 1. 63, in *The Poetical Works,* ed. C. B. Tinker and H. F. Lowry (London, 1950), p. 272.

18. *Ibid.*, pp. 271–272. Of the quoted phrases, the first occurs in 1. 67, and the third in 1. 46. The second occurs in lines suppressed after the poem's first appearance in print. See p. 271 n.

19. *Wordsworth's Literary Criticism*, (London, 1905), p. 17.

20. Roy Pascal, *Design and Truth in Autobiography* (Cambridge, Mass., 1960), p. 82.

21. *Ibid.*, p. viii.

22. *Sartor Resartus*, p. 149.

PART II

1. *Autobiography of Roger North*, p. 169.
2. *Ibid.*, p. 11.
3. *Ibid.*, pp. 28–29.
4. James L. Clifford, ed., *Biography as an Art: Selected Criticism 1560–1960* (New York, 1962), p. xii.
5. *Ibid.*, p. 31.
6. *Lives*, III, 273.
7. Clifford, *Biography*, p. 27.
8. *Ibid.*, p. 32.
9. *Ibid.*, p. 29.
10. *Lives*, II, 421.
11. *Ibid.*, I, 153–154.
12. *Ibid.*, II, 99–100.
13. Clifford, *Biography*, p. 34.
14. *Lives*, I, 8.
15. John Toland, "The Life of John Milton," in *The Early Lives of Milton*, ed. Helen Darbishire (London, 1932), pp. 83–84.
16. *Boswell's Life of Johnson*, ed. George Birkbeck Hill and revised and enlarged by L. F. Powell (Oxford, 1934), I, 33.
17. *Lives*, III, 201.
18. *Autobiography of Roger North*, p. 67.
19. *Ibid.*, p. 166.
20. *Lives*, I, 193.
21. *Ibid.*, II, 253.
22. *Autobiography of Roger North*, p. 86.
23. *Ibid.*, p. 166.
24. *Lives*, II, 88.
25. *Ibid.*, II, 223–224.
26. *Ibid.*, I, 309–310.
27. *Ibid.*, pp. 350–351.

28. *Ibid.*, III, 370.
29. *Ibid.*, p. 336.
30. *Ibid.*, p. 98.
31. *Ibid.*, p. 223.
32. *Ibid.*, I, 147.
33. *Ibid.*, I, 39–40.
34. *Ibid.*, II, 232.
35. *Autobiography of Roger North*, pp. 32–33.
36. *Lives*, III, 220.
37. *Ibid.*, pp. 94–95.
38. *Ibid.*, p. 96.
39. *Ibid.*, II, 381.
40. *Ibid.*, III, 121.
41. *Ibid.*, p. 213.
42. *Ibid.*, p. 216.
43. *loc. cit.*
44. *Ibid.*, p. 219.
45. *Ibid.*, II, 179.
46. *Ibid.*, III, 299–301.
47. *Ibid.*, p. 209.
48. *Ibid.*, p. 210.
49. *Autobiography of Roger North*, p. 64.
50. *Ibid.*, p. 16.
51. *Ibid.*, p. 35.
52. *Ibid.*, p. 26.
53. *Ibid.*, pp. 25 26.
54. *Ibid.*, p. 65.
55. *Lives*, II, 180.
56. *Ibid.*, pp. 201–202.
57. *History of the Royal Society*, ed. Jackson I. Cope and Harold Whitmore Jones (St. Louis, 1958), p. 76.
58. *Autobiography of Roger North*, p. 21.
59. *loc. cit.*
60. *Ibid.*, p. 70.
61. *Ibid.*, pp. 68–69.
62. *Ibid.*, p. 73.
63. *Ibid.*, p. 8.
64. *Ibid.*, p. 9.
65. *Ibid.*, pp. 9–10.
66. *Lives*, I, 274.
67. *Ibid.*, pp. 274–275.
68. *Ibid.*, pp. 275–276.
69. *Ibid.*, p. 276.

70. *Ibid.*, p. 99.
71. *Ibid.*, II, 42–43.
72. *Ibid.*, p. 44.
73. *Autobiography of Roger North*, p. 104.
74. *Ibid.*, p. 21.
75. Lytton Strachey, *Portraits in Miniature and Other Essays* (New York, 1962), p. 152.
76. John Murray, ed., *The Autobiographies of Edward Gibbon* (London, 1897). The lettering of the fragments in my text is Murray's.
77. George Birkbeck Hill, ed., *The Memoirs of Edward Gibbon* (London, 1900), p. x.
78. Donald Stauffer, *The Art of Biography in Eighteenth-Century England* (Princeton, 1941), p. 370.
79. Hill, *op cit.*, p. vi.
80. Edward Gibbon, *Autobiography*, introd. Oliphant Smeaton (London, 1911), p. x.
81. Hill, *op. cit.*, p. ix.
82. Roy Pascal, *Design and Truth in Autobiography*, (Cambridge, Mass., 1960), p. 38.

PART III

1. Louella M. Wright, *The Literary Life of the Early Friends* (New York, 1932), p. 110; and Thomas Jackson, *Lives of Early Methodist Preachers* (1838), III, iii, quoted in Donald Stauffer, *The Art of Biography in Eighteenth-Century England* (Princeton, 1941), p. 260.
2. F. J. Sheed, trans., *The Confessions of St. Augustine* (New York, 1942), p. 185.
3. Lionel Trilling, *The Liberal Imagination: Essays on Literature and Society* (London, 1951), pp. 179–180.
4. Sigmund Freud, *The Interpretation of Dreams*, trans. James Strachey (New York, 1955), pp. 394–395.
5. William James, *The Varieties of Religious Experience*, (London and New York, 1902), pp. 144, 157.
6. *Ibid.*, pp. 159, 187.
7. Norman O. Brown, *Life against Death: The Psychoanalytical Meaning of History* (Middletown, Conn., 1959).
8. James Dickinson, *A Journal of the Life, Travels, and Labour of Love of That Worthy Elder, and Faithful Servant of Christ, James Dickinson* (London, 1745), p. 63.
9. *Ibid.*, p. 11.

10. *Ibid.*, p. 8.
11. *Ibid.*, p. 9.
12. *The Journal and a Plea for the Poor* (New York, 1961), p. 221.
13. *Ibid.*, pp. 48–49.
14. *Ibid.*, pp. 8–9.
15. *Ibid.*, p. 8.
16. *Ibid.*, p. 214.
17. *Ibid.*, p. 215.
18. Thomas Ellwood, *The History of the Life of Thomas Ellwood* (4th ed.; London, 1791).
19. David Ferris, *Memoirs of the Life of David Ferris* (Philadelphia, 1855).
20. *An Extract of Miss Mary Gilbert's Journal* (6th ed.; London, 1813), p. 6.
21. *Ibid.*, pp. 11, 15.
22. *Ibid.*, p. 22.
23. *Ibid.*, p. 8.
24. *Ibid.*, p. 49.
25. Donald Stauffer, *The Art of Biography in Eighteenth-Century England* (Princeton, 1941), p. 260.
26. *A Short Account of God's Dealings with the Reverend George Whitefield, A.B.* (London, 1740), p. 7.
27. *Ibid.*, p. 30.
28. *Ibid.*, p. 37.
29. *Ibid.*, p. 40.
30. *Ibid.*, pp. 47, 49.
31. *A Short Account of God's Dealings with Mr. John Haime* (London, 1810).
32. *Ibid.*, p. 6.
33. *Ibid.*, p. 1.
34. *Ibid.*, p. 6.
35. *Ibid.*, p. 5.
36. *loc. cit.*
37. *Ibid.*, p. 9.
38. *Ibid.*, p. 11.
39. *loc. cit.*
40. *Ibid.*, p. 15.
41. *Ibid.*, pp. 19–20.
42. *Ibid.*, p. 23.
43. *Ibid.*, p. 24.
44. *Ibid.*, p. 30.
45. *Ibid.*, pp. 30–31.
46. *Ibid.*, p. 35.

47. *An Account of the Life and Dealings of God with Silas Told, Late Preacher of the Gospel* (London, 1808), p. 87.

48. *Ibid.*, pp. 7–9.

49. *Ibid.*, p. 38.

50. *Ibid.*, p. 93.

51. *Ibid.*, pp. 23–24.

52. *Ibid.*, p. 69.

53. *Ibid.*, p. 70.

54. *Ibid.*, pp. 12–13.

55. *Ibid.*, p. 62.

56. *Ibid.*, pp. 64–65.

57. *Ibid.*, p. 65.

58. *loc. cit.*

59. *Ibid.*, pp. 84–85.

60. *Ibid.*, p. 85.

61. *loc. cit.*

62. *Ibid.*, p. 86.

63. *loc. cit.*

64. *Ibid.*, p. 87.

65. *loc. cit.*

66. Donald Stauffer, *op. cit.*, p. 303.

67. John Stuart Mill, *On Bentham and Coleridge*, p. 63.

68. Charles Ryskamp, *William Cowper of the Middle Temple: A Study of His Life and Works to the Year 1768* (Cambridge, 1959), p. 67.

69. *Ibid.*, p. 83.

70. *Ibid.*, pp. 150–152.

71. Sigmund Freud, *The Complete Psychological Works*, trans. James Strachey (London, 1960), VI, 279.

72. William Cowper, *Poetical Works* (London, 1926), p. 432.

73. Lionel Trilling, *op. cit.*, pp. 179–180.

PART IV

1. Roy Pascal, *Design and Truth in Autobiography* (Cambridge, Mass., 1960), p. 3.

2. *Boswell on the Grand Tour: Italy, Corsica, and France, 1765–1766*, ed. Frank Brady and Frederick A. Pottle (New York, 1955), p. xix. Hereafter, this volume will be cited as *Italy, Corsica, and France*.

3. Northrop Frye, "Towards Defining an Age of Sensibility," in James L. Clifford, ed., *Eighteenth-Century English Literature: Modern Essays in Criticism* (New York, 1959), p. 312.

NOTES

4. *loc. cit.*

5. *The Rise of the Novel: Studies in Defoe, Richardson, and Fielding* (Berkeley and Los Angeles, 1957), pp. 191–192.

6. *Ibid.*, p. 292.

7. *Boswell: The Ominous Years, 1774–1776*, ed. Charles Ryskamp and Frederick A. Pottle (New York, 1963), p. 54. Hereafter, this volume will be cited as *Ominous Years*.

8. *Italy, Corsica, and France*, p. 228.

9. *Ominous Years*, p. 250.

10. *Ibid.*, p. 54.

11. *Boswell's Journal of a Tour to the Hebrides with Samuel Johnson, LL.D., 1773*, ed. Frederick A. Pottle and Charles H. Bennett, new edition with additional notes by Frederick A. Pottle (New York, 1962), p. 346. Hereafter, this volume will be cited as *Hebrides*.

12. *Private Papers of James Boswell from Malahide Castle*, ed. Geoffrey Scott and Frederick A. Pottle (Mt. Vernon, N.Y., 1928–1934), X, xi. Hereafter this work will be cited as *Private Papers*.

13. *Hebrides*.

14. *Boswell in Search of a Wife, 1766–1769*, ed. Frank Brady and Frederick A. Pottle (New York, 1956), p. 292. Hereafter, this volume will be cited as *Wife*.

15. *Italy, Corsica, and France*, p. 22.

16. *Boswell's London Journal, 1762–1763*, ed. Frederick A. Pottle (New York, 1950), p. 241. Hereafter, this volume will be cited as *London*.

17. *Italy, Corsica, and France*, p. 276.

18. *Ominous Years*, p. 101.

19. *London*, p. 286.

20. *Ominous Years*, pp. 272–273.

21. *Italy, Corsica, and France*, p. 41.

22. *loc. cit.*

23. *Wife*, p. 242.

24. *Ominous Years*, p. 293.

25. *loc. cit.*

26. *Design and Truth in Autobiography*, p. 182.

27. *Private Papers*, XVII, 25.

28. *Ominous Years*, p. x.

29. *Ibid.*, pp. 286–287.

30. *Ibid.*, pp. 304–307.

31. *Ibid.*, p. 316.

32. *Ibid.*, p. 322.

33. *Ibid.*, p. 323 n.

34. *Ibid.*, p. 192.

35. *London*, p. 89.

36. *Ibid.*, pp. 96–98.
37. *Ibid.*, p. 97.
38. *Ibid.*, p. 117.
39. *Ibid.*, p. 140.
40. *Ibid.*, p. 161.
41. Frederick S. Kiley, "Boswell's Literary Art in the *London Journal*," *College English*, XXIII (1962), 632.
42. *London*, p. 13 n.
43. W. H. Auden, "Young Boswell," *The New Yorker*, XXVI (November 25, 1950), 147.
44. *Ominous Years*, p. 243.
45. *London*, p. 303.
46. *Hebrides*, p. 165.
47. *Boswell on the Grand Tour: Germany and Switzerland, 1764*, ed. Frederick A. Pottle (New York, 1953), p. 58. Hereafter, this volume will be cited as *Germany and Switzerland.*
48. *Ibid.*, pp. 143–144.
49. *Ominous Years*, p. 220.
50. *Ibid.*, p. 240.
51. *London*, p. 283.
52. *Germany and Switzerland*, p. 252.
53. *Ominous Years*, p. 174.
54. *Ibid.*, p. 286.
55. *Germany and Switzerland*, p. 212.
56. *Ominous Years*, p. 6.
57. *Ibid.*, p. 265.
58. *Boswell for the Defense, 1769–1774*, ed. William K. Wimsatt, Jr. (New York, 1959), p. 279. Hereafter, this volume will be cited as *Defense.*
59. *Ominous Years*, pp. 174–175.
60. *Ibid.*, p. 171.
61. *Boswell in Holland, 1763–1764*, ed. Frederick A. Pottle (New York, 1952), pp. 239, 190. Hereafter, this volume will be cited as *Holland.*
62. *Germany and Switzerland*, p. 22.
63. *Ibid.*, pp. 53–54.
64. *Ibid.*, p. 54.
65. *Defense*, p. 100.
66. *Wife*, p. 141.
67. *Private Papers*, XVIII, 220.
68. *London*, p. 252 n.
69. *Ibid.*, p. 251.
70. *Ibid.*, pp. 263–264.
71. *Ibid.*, pp. 272–273.
72. Kiley, *op. cit.*, pp. 631–632.

73. For a brief account of her, see the introduction to Boswell's correspondence with her, in *Holland,* pp. 293–297.
74. See the Editorial Note in *Ominous Years,* pp. 352–355.
75. *London,* p. 84.
76. *Ibid.,* p. 241.
77. *Ibid.,* p. 126.
78. *Wife,* p. 237.
79. *Ibid.,* p. 236.
80. *Ibid.,* p. 239.
81. *Ominous Years,* p. 188.
82. *London,* p. 134.
83. *The Second Part of King Henry the Fourth,* ed. Samuel B. Hemingway (New Haven, 1921), IV, v, 11. 118–130, 150–153.
84. *Ominous Years,* p. 230.
85. *Germany and Switzerland,* p. 29.
86. *Wife,* p. xi.
87. *Ominous Years,* p. xvii.
88. *Ibid.,* p. 86.
89. *Wife.* p. 96.
90. *Hebrides,* p. 160.
91. *Ibid.,* p. 336.
92. *Ominous Years,* p. 53.
93. *Ibid.,* p. 186.
94. *Ibid.,* p. 206.
95. *Ibid.,* p. xvii.
96. *Ibid.,* p. 7.
97. *Private Papers,* XVIII, 19.
98. *London,* p. 161.
99. *loc. cit.*

PART V

1. "Preface to Shakespeare," in *The Works of Samuel Johnson* (Troy, N.Y., 1903), XII, 9.
2. James H. Smith and Edd W. Parks, eds., *The Great Critics* (New York, 1951), p. 31.
3. Roy Pascal, *Design and Truth in Autobiography,* (Cambridge, Mass., 1960), p. 38.
4. *Autobiography,* (New York, 1924), p. 95.
5. *On Bentham and Coleridge,* (London, 1950), p. 63.
6. *Anti-Intellectualism in American Life* (New York, 1963), pp. 55–141.

7. Donald Malcolm, "The Underside of the Tapestry," *The New Yorker*, XXXIX (January 25, 1964), 106.

8. *Autobiography*, p. 100.

9. Hyder Edward Rollins, ed., *The Letters of John Keats* (Cambridge, Mass., 1958), II, 102.

Acknowledgments

The author wishes to express his gratitude to the following:

American Philosophical Society for permission to reprint from Maurice J. Quinlan, "Memoir of William Cowper—An Autobiography," *American Philosophical Society Proceedings*, 97 (1953).

Cambridge University Press for permission to reprint from Charles Ryskamp, *William Cowper of the Middle Temple;* and John L. Nickalls, ed., *The Journal of George Fox.*

The Clarendon Press, Oxford, for permission to reprint from William Wordsworth, *The Prelude*, ed. by Ernest de Selincourt, 2nd rev. ed., Helen Darbishire, 1959; and James Boswell, *Life of Johnson*, ed. by G. B. Hill, Vol. I, 1934.

Columbia University Press for permission to reprint from *The Autobiography of John Stuart Mill*, 1924.

Harvard University Press for permission to reprint from Roy Pascal, *Design and Truth in Autobiography*, 1960.

McGraw-Hill for permission to reprint from *Boswell on the Grand Tour: Italy, Corsica and France*, ed. by Frank Brady and Frederick A. Pottle, © 1955 by Yale University; *Boswell: The Ominous Years*, ed. by Charles Ryskamp and Frederick A. Pottle, © 1963 by Yale University; *Boswell's Journal of a Tour to the Hebrides with Samuel Johnson*, ed. by Frederick A. Pottle and Charles H. Bennett, © 1961 by Yale University; *Boswell in Search of a Wife*, ed. by Frank Brady and Frederick A. Pottle, © 1956 by Yale University; *Boswell's London Journal*, ed. by Frederick A. Pottle, © 1950 by Yale University; *Boswell on the Grand Tour: Germany and Switzerland*, ed.

by Frederick A. Pottle, © 1953 by Yale University; *Boswell for the Defense*, ed. by William K. Wimsatt, Jr., © 1959; and *Boswell in Holland*, ed. by Frederick A. Pottle, © 1952 by Yale University.

The Editors and the publisher, National Psychological Association for Psychoanalysis, New York, for permission to reprint from A. S. Levi, "The Mental Crisis of John Stuart Mill," *The Psychoanalytic Review*, 32 (Spring 1945), No. 1.

Oxford University Press for permission to reprint from James F. Clifford, *Biography as an Art*.

The University of California Press for permission to reprint from Ian Watt, *Studies in DeFoe, Richardson, and Fielding*, pp. 191–192.

The Viking Press for permission to reprint from Lionel Trilling, "Wordsworth and the Rabbis," *The Opposing Self*, copyright 1950 by Lionell Trilling.

The World Publishing Company for permission to quote from the following Meridian Book: Dero H. Saunders, ed., *The Autobiography of Edward Gibbon*, 1961.

INDEX

INDEX

INDEX

DUE